K Hee

Legends of the
American Indians

Legends of the American Indians

Text by
Henry Rowe-Schoolcraft

Crescent Books
New York

First English edition published by
Editions Minerva S.A., Genève.
Copyright © MCMLXXX
by Editions Minerva S.A., Genève.
All rights reserved.

Library of Congress Catalog Card
Number: 79-57030
ISBN: 0-517-307065

This edition is published by Crescent Books,
a division of Crown Publishers, Inc.

a b c d e f g h
Printed in Italy

Contents

Introduction

The following tales are published as specimens of an oral imaginative lore existing among the North American aborigines. In the long period of time in which these tribes have been subjects of observation, we are not aware that powers of this kind have been attributed to them. And it may be asked: Why the discovery of this peculiar trait in their intellectual character has not been made until the first quarter of the nineteenth century? The force of the query is acknowledged; and, in asserting the claim for them, the writer of these pages proposes first to offer to the public some proofs of the correctness of his own conclusions on this point.

The era of the discovery was the era of maritime adventure. The master spirits of those times were men of shrewd, keen sense and adventurous tempers, who wished to get ahead in the world, and relied for their success, rather upon the compass and sword, than upon their pens. It was the age of action and not of research. Least of all, had they the means or the inclination to inquire into the mental capacities of fierce and warlike races of hunters and warriors, who claimed to be lords of the soil, and actually exterminated the first settle-

ment made in St. Domingo and in Virginia. They set out from Europe with a lamentable want of true information respecting them, and were disappointed in not finding them wild animals on two legs. Long after the discovery, it was debated whether any faith ought to be kept with them; and the chief point of inquiry was, not whether they had any right to the soil, but how they could be turned to the best account in the way of trade and merchandise. The Spaniards, who occupy the foreground in the career of discovery, began by selling the Indian and compelling him to feudal servitude, and would probably have driven as profitable a traffic as was subsequently carried on with the Africans, had it not soon appeared that the Indian was a lazy man, and not a productive labourer. He sank under the overwhelming idea of hopeless servitude, lingered a few years an unprofitable miner, and died. The project was therefore relinquished, not because of the awakened sensibilities of the conquerors, but because it was (in the mercantile acceptation of the term) a bad business. The history of the manners, customs, and languages of the ancient nations, and particularly of the oriental branches of the human family, from whom they were thought to have descended, was deeply in the dark. Comparative philology was unknown, and the spirit of critical and historical acumen, which has evinced itself in Germany in modern days, and is rapidly extending itself over the world, still slumbered under the intellectual darkness which spellbound the human mind after the overthrow of Greece and Rome, and the dispersion of the Jews. To expect, therefore, that the hardy commanders of exploring voyages should have, at the opening of the sixteenth century, entered into any minute inquiries of the kind referred to, would be to expect that the human mind should reverse its ordinary mode of operation. These men do not appear to have troubled themselves with the inquiry whether the Indians had a history: certainly they took no pains to put on record facts in the department of inquiry to which our attention is now directed. This view results from an attentive examination of the earlier voyages and histories of adventure in this hemisphere, in which is exhibited the coldest air of mercantile calculation. The journals themselves are mere logbooks, rigid and dry in their details, destitute of any powers of reflection upon the events they narrate, and unrelieved by exact research, tact of observation, or high-souled sentiment.

History is required to pass a less censorious judgment on the moral character of those of the colonists who settled north of the latitudes of the West Indies. The great Anglo-Saxon stock, which spread along the shores of the North Atlantic, carried with it notions of liberty and justice, which shielded the aboriginal tribes from the curse of slavery. They treated them as having a just right to the occupancy of the soil, and formed treaties with them. They acknowledged, by the acts, their existence as independent political communities, and maintained, in their fullest extent, the doctrine of political faith and responsability. Some of the colonies went farther, and early directed their attention to their improvement and conversion to Christianity. The two powers were, however, placed in circumstances adverse to the prosperous and contemporaneous growth of both, while they occupied a territory over which there was a disputed sovereignty. It must needs have happened, that the party which increased the fastest, in numbers, wanted most land, and had most knowledge (to say nothing of the influence of temperance and virtue), should triumph, and those who failed in these requisites, decline. It is believed that this is the true cause why the transplanted European race overspread the land, and the Indians were driven before them. And that the result is by no means owing to a proper want of sympathy for the latter, or of exertions both to better their condition and avert their fate. The Indians could not, however, be made to understand this. They did not look to causes, but reasoned wholly from effects. They saw the white race occupying the prominent harbours, pushing up the navigable streams, spreading over the uplands, and multiplying in numbers "like sands on the seashore." And they attributed to hostile purpose, breach of faith, and cupidity, what was, to a very great extent, owing to their own idle habits, vices, and short-sightedness. The two races soon came to measure swords; and this contest extended, with short periods of intervening peace, from about A.D. 1600 to the close of 1814. The Indians staked stratagem and the geographical obstacles of a vast unknown wilderness, against knowledge, resources, and discipline. Their policy was to fly when pursued, and pursue when relieved from pursuit; to avoid field fights, and carry on a most harassing war of detail. By avoiding concentration in camps, and occupying a comparatively large area of country, they have compelled their assailants, at all times, to employ a force entirely disproportioned to that required to cope with the same number of civilized troops. The result of this long-continued, and often renewed contest for supremacy, it is only necessary to advert to. It has been anything but favourable to the production of right feelings and a reciprocal knowledge of real character on both sides. The Indians could never be made to appreciate the offers of education and Christianity by one portion of the community, while others, were arrayed against them in arms. Their idea of government was, after all, the Eastern notion of a unity or despotism, in which everything emanates from the governing power, and is responsible to it. Nor has their flitting and feverish position on the frontiers been auspicious to the acquisition of a true knowledge of their character, particularly in those things which have relation of the Indian mind, their opinions on abstract subjects, their mythology, and other kindred topics. Owing to illitterate interpreters and dishonest men, the parties have never more than half understood each other. Distrust and misapprehension have existed by the century together. And it is, therefore, no cause for astonishment, that the whole period of our contemporaneous history should be filled up with so many negotiations and cessions, wars and treaties.

These remarks are offered to indicate, that the several periods of our colonial and confederate history, and wars, were unfavourable to the acquisition of that species of information respecting their mental capacities and social institutions, of which it is our purpose to speak. The whole tendency of our intercourse with them has been, to demonstrate rather the physical than moral capabilities of the Indian, his expertness in war, his skill, stratagem, powers of endurance, and contempt of suffering. Indian fortitude has been applauded at the stake, and Indian kindness and generosity acknowledged in the wigwam, and in the mazes of the wilderness. Admiration had been excited

11

by his noble sentiments of independence and exaltation above personal fear. Above all, perhaps, had he been accredited for intellect in his acuteness in negotiation and the simple force of his oratory. But the existence of an intellectual invention had never been traced, so far as it is known, to the amusements of his domestic fireside; nor could it well have been conjectured to occupy so wide a field for its display in legendary tales and fables.

My attention was first arrested by the fact of the existence of such tales among the Odjibwa nation inhabiting the region about Lake Superior in 1822. Two years previous, I had gone out in that quarter as one of the members of a corps of observation, on an exploratory expedition to the head waters of the Mississippi. The large area of territory which it was found this tribe occupied, together with their number and warlike character, induced the department of war to extend a military post to the Falls or Sault of St. Mary's, near the outlet of Lake Superior, in the year above named. I accompanied this force, and assumed, at the same time, an official relation to this tribe, as Agent of Indian Affairs, which led me to inquire into their distinctive history, language, and characteristic traits. It was found that they possessed a story-telling faculty, and I wrote down from their narration a number of these fictitious tales; some of which were amusing merely, others were manifestly intended to convey mythologic or allegoric information. The boundaries between truth and fiction are but feebly defined among the aborigines of this Continent, and it was found in this instance, that the individuals of the tribe who related the tales were also the depositories of their historical traditions, such as they were; and these narrators wove the few and scattered incidents and landmarks of their history into the web and woof of their wildest tales. I immediately announced this interesting discovery in their moral character to a few friends and correspondents, who were alike interest in the matter; and a new zest was thus given to the inquiry, and the field of observation greatly extended. The result was the finding of similar tales among all the northwestern tribes whose traditions were investigated. They were also found among some of the tribes west of the Mississippi, and the present state of the inquiry demonstrates that this species of oral lore is common to the Algic, the Ostic, and some tribes of the Abanic stock. It is conjectured to exist among the rather extended branches of the Muskogee, and also the Cherokee, although no actual proof is possessed. And it becomes a question of interest to ascertain how far a similar trait can be traced among the North American tribes, and where the exceptions and limitations are to be found. To find a trait which must hereafter be deemed characteristic of the mental habits of these tribes, so diffused, furnishes a strong motive for extending inquiries farther and wider. It may be asked whether the South American aborigines possessed or still possess, this point of intellectual affinity with the tribes of the North. Did Manco Capac and Montezuma employ this means to strengthen political power, inspire courage, or console themselves under misfortune? Do the ice-bound and impoverished natives of the Artic circle draw inspiration in their cruel vicissitudes from a similar intellectual source? What sound deductions can be drawn from a comparison of Eastern with Western fable, as thus developed? And, finally, is this propensity connected, in other of the American stock tribes, with a hieroglyphic system of notation, as we find it in the Algic, which will bear any useful comparison with the phonetic system of Egypt, the Runic of Iceland and Norway, or with any other mode of perpetuating the knowledge of events or things known to the human race?

A few remarks may be added respecting the character of the tales now submitted to inspection. And the first is, that they appear to be of a homogeneous and vernacular origin. There are distinctive tribal traits, but the general features coincide. The ideas and incidents do not appear to be borrowed or unnatural. The situations and circumstances are such as are common to the people. The language and phraseology are of the most simple kind. Few adjectives are used, and few comparisons resorted to. The style of narration, the cast of invention, the theory of thinking, are eminently peculiar to a people who wander about in woods and plains, who encounter wild beasts, believe in demons, and are subject to the vicissitudes of the seasons. The tales refer themselves to a people who are polytheists; not believers in one God or Great Spirit, but of thousands of spirits; a people who live in fear, who wander in want, and who die in misery. The machinery of spirits and necromancy, one of the most ancient and prevalent errors of the human race, supplies the framework of these fictitious creations. Language to carry out the conceptions might seem to be wanting, but here the narrator finds a ready resource in the use of metaphor, the doctrine of metamorphosis, and the personification of inanimate objects; for the latter of which, the grammar of the language has a peculiar adaptation. Deficiencies of the vocabulary are thus supplied, life and action are imparted to the whole material creation, and every purpose of description is answered. The belief of the narrators and listeners in every wild and improbable thing told, helps wonderfully, in the original, in joining the sequence of parts together. Nothing is too capacious for Indian belief. Almost every declaration is a prophecy, and every tale a creed. He believes that the whole visible and invisible creation is animated with various orders of malignant or benign spirits, who preside over the daily affairs and over the final destinies of men. He believes that these spirits must be conciliated by sacrifices, and a series of fasts and feasts either follow or precede these rites, that by the one they may be rendered acceptable, and by the other, his gratitude may be shown. This constitutes the groundwork of the Algic religion: but superstition has ingrafted upon the original stock, till the growth is a upas of giant size, bearing the bitter fruits of demonology, witchcraft, and necromancy. To make the matter worse, these tribes believe that animals of the lowest, as well as highest class in the chain of creation, are alike endowed with reasoning powers and faculties. And as a natural conclusion, they endow birds, and bears, and all other animals with souls, which, they believe, will be encountered in other shapes in another state of existence. So far the advantages of actual belief come in aid of their fictitious creations, and this is the true cause why so much importance is attached to the flight and appearance of particular birds, who being privileged to ascend in the air, are supposed by them to be conversant with the wishes, or to act in obedience to the mandates of the spirits; and the circumstance of this belief deserves to be borne in mind in the perusal of their tales, as it will be found that the words put into the mouths, of the actors express the actual opinions of the natives on life, death, and immortality, topics which have heretofore been impenetrably veiled.

The value of these traditionary stories appeared to depend, very much, upon their being left, as nearly as possible, in their original forms of thought and expression. In the original there is no attempt at ornament. Great attention is paid, in the narration, to repeating the conversations and speeches, and imitating the very tone and gesture of the actors. This is sometimes indulged at the risk of tautology. Moral point has been given to no tale which does not, in the original, justify it; and it is one of the unlooked-for features connected with the subject, that so considerable a proportion of them possess this trait. It is due to myself, and to those who have aided me in the collection and translation of the materials, to say, that the advantages enjoyed in this respect have been of the most favourable character. The whole examination, extending, with intervals, through a period of seventeen years, has been conducted not only with the aid that a public station, as an executive officer for the tribes, has supplied, but with the superadded intelligence and skill in the languages existing within the range of my domestic and affiliated circle.

Of the antiquity of the tales, the surest external evidence may probably be drawn from the lexicography. In a language in which the actor and the object are riveted, so to speak, by transitive inflections, it must needs happen that the history of its names for objects, whether preserved orally or by letters, is, in fact, the history of the introduction of the objects named, and this fixes eras in the enlargement of the vocabulary. Although it is true, that without letters these eras cannot be accurately fixed, yet valuable inferences may be drawn from an examination of this branch of the inquiry. Words are like coins, and may, like them, be examined to illustrate history. It has been found that those of the highest antiquity are simple and brief. Most of the primitive nouns are monosyllabic, and denote but a single object or idea. A less number are dissyllabic; few exceed this; and it may be questioned, from the present state of the examination, whether there is a single primitive trisyllable. The primitives become polysyllabic by adding an inflection indicating the presence or absence of vitality (which is the succedaneum for gender), and a farther inflection to denote number. They also admit of adjective terminations. Pronouns are denoted by particles prefixed or suffixed. The genius of the language is accumulative, and tends rather to add syllables or letters, making farther distinctions in objects already before the mind, than to introduce new words. A simple word is thus oftentimes converted into a descriptive phrase, at once formidable to the eye and the ear. And it is only by dissecting such compounds that the radix can be attained.

Judged by this test, most of the tales are of the era of flint arrow-heads, earthen pots, and skin clothes. Their fish-nets are represented as being made of the bark of trees. No mention is made of a blanket, gun, knife, or any metallic instrument; we do not hear of their cutting down trees, except in a single instance, yet there is nothing to indicate that their economical labours were not well performed. Au is an original, causitive particle, and appears to be the root of a numerous class of words, sometimes with, and sometimes without a consonant added. Aukee is earth, and may be. By adding k to this root the term is made specific, and denotes an earthen pot or kettle. Aubik is the radix for metal, ore, rock. By prefixing the particle Pe, we have the name for iron, Misk for copper, and so forth; but as euphony requires, in forming compounds, that two vowels should not come together, the sound of w is inter-posed in these particular instances. Gunzh is the radix for plant; Tig for tree; Asee for animal; and either by suffixing or prefixing syllabical increments, the terminology of the three great departments of nature is formed. The terms of consanguinity are derived from Ai, a heart, hence Si-ai, elder brother, Sheem-ai, younger brother, or younger sister. Konaus, a loose wrapper, in the most ancient and genetic term for a garment which has been found. The principal female garment, leggon, are derivatives from it. Muttataus, a beaver robe, is from the same root. Wyaun, a furred skin, and Waigin, a dressed skin, appear to form the bases of the nomenclature for the Indian wardrobe. Blanket is a modern term, meaning white furred skin. Woollen cloth took the name of dressed skin, and its various colours and qualities are indicated by adjective

16

prefixes. Calicoes or printed cottons are named from a generic, meaning speckled or spotted. All these are modern terms, as modern as those for a horse, a sheep, or a hog, and, like the latter, are descriptive and polysyllabic. Tobacco and the zea mays, both indigenous productions, are mentioned. The latter is the subject of a simple allegoric tale.

These particulars may suffice to indicate the importance of etymological analysis in examining the antiquity of the tales. Narrations of a later era are denoted by the introduction of the modern compounds, such as their names for the domestic animals of Europe, a gun, a rifle, a ship, a spyglass, compass, watch, hat. The bow and arrow, club and lance, are the only species of arms actually described as in use, except in a single instance, and this tale is manifestly an interpolated version of an ancient story. The father of the winds makes battle with a huge flagroot, and the king of reptiles is shot with a dart.

Geographical terms and allusions to the climate supply another branch of comparison. Some of the grand features of the country are referred to by their modern Indian names, but this is nearly restricted to what may be termed the historical legends. There are frequent allusions to the Northern hemisphere. Snow, ice, and lakes are referred to. Warm latitudes are once or twice mentioned, and the allusions are coupled with admonitions against the danger of corrupt and effeminate manners and habits.

Astronomy and cosmogony constitute subjects of frequent notice; and this might naturally be expected from a people who are quick in their perceptions of external nature, and pass a large share of their time under the open sky. The phenomena of thunder, lightning, the aurora borealis, meteors, the rainbow, the galaxy of the milky way, the morning and evening stars, and the more prominent groups of the fixed and minor stars, are specifically named and noticed. The cardinal points are accurately distinguished. They entertain the semi-ancient theory that the earth is spheroidal, and the sun and moon perform their circuits round it. The visiters to these luminaries, described in the text, personify the former as a male and the latter as a female, under the idea of brother and sister. We are left to infer, from another passage, that they believe the sky revolves. Nothing, however, in the "open firmament", is a subject of more constant and minute observation, and a more complex terminology, than the clouds. Their colour, shape, transparency or obscurity, movements, and relative position to the sun and to each other, constitute objects of minute notice and deep importance. A large proportion of the names of individuals in the Algic tribes is drawn from this fruitful source of Indian observation. The Great Spirit is invariably located in the sky, and the Evil Spirit, and the train of minor malignant Spirits, in the earth. Their notions of the position of seas and continents are altogether vague and confused. Nor has it been observed that they have any knowledge of volcanic action. The idea of a universal deluge appears to be equally entertained by the tribes of North and South America. The Algics certainly have it incorporated in their traditionary tales, and I have found the belief in these traditions, the most firmly seated among the bands the farthest removed from the advances of civilization and Christianity.

It is the mythology, however, of these tribes which affords the deepest insight into their character, and unfolds, perhaps, some of the clearest coincidences with Oriental rites and opinions. Were the terms Baalim and Magii introduced into the descriptions of their worship, instead of Manito and Meeta, his coincidence would be very apparent. Medical magic spread the charms of its delusion over the semi-barbaric tribes who, at a very early epoch, spread from the Persian and the Arabian Gulfs to the Mediterranean; and it would not be a light task to find branches of the human race who are more completely characterized by its doctrines and practices than the wide-spreading members of the Algic stock of this Continent. Their prophets, jugglers, and meetays occupy the same relative importance in the political scale. They advise the movement of armies, and foretell the decrees of fate to individuals. They interpret dreams, affect the performance of miraculous cures, and preside over the most sacred rites. Oracles alike to chiefs and kings, warriors and hunters, nothing can be accomplished without their aid, and it would be presumptuous and impious to attempt anything, in war or peace, which they had decreed to be

18

wrong. But our more immediate object is the class of oral fictions among the Western tribes, and for the growth and development of which their peculiar belief in the doctrine of spirits and magicians has furnished so wide a field. Come from what quarter of the world they may, the propensity to amusing and serio-comic fiction appears to have been brought with them. What traits, if any, of the original threadwork of foreign story remain, it would be premature, in the present state of these collections, to decide. The character and incidents of the narrations are adapted to the condition they are now in, as well as the position they now occupy. There is, it is true, a spirit of reminiscence apparent which pleases itself in allusions to the past; they speak of a sort of golden age, when all things were better with them than they now are; when they had better laws and leaders; when crimes were more promptly punished; when their language was spoken with greater purity, and their manners were freer from barbarism. But all this seems to flit through the Indian mind as a dream, and furnishes him rather the source of a pleasing secret retrospection than any spring to present and future exertions. He pines away as one that is fallen, and despairs to rise. He does not seem to open his eyes on the prospect of civilization and mental exaltation held up before him, as one to whom the scene is new or attractive. These scenes have been pictured before him by teachers and philanthropists for more than two centuries; but there has been nothing in them to arouse and inspire him to press onward in the career of prospective civilization and refinement. He has rather turned away with the air of one to whom all things "new" were "old", and chosen emphatically to re-embrace his woods, his wigwam, and his canoe.

Perhaps the trait that was least to have been anticipated in the tales is the moral often conveyed by them. But, on reflection, this is in accordance with the Indian maxim, which literally requires "an eye for an eye, and a tooth for a tooth." And the more closely this feature of poetic justice is scrutinized, the more striking does it appear. Cruelty, murder, and sorcery are eventually punished, although the individual escapes for the time and his career may be long drawn out. Domestic infidelity meets the award of death in the only instance narrated.

Religious vows are held inviolate. Respect for parents and for age, fraternal affection, hospitality, bravery, self-denial, endurance under fatigue or suffering, and disinterestedness, are uniformly inculcated. Presumption and pride are rebuked, and warnings given against the allurements of luxury and its concomitant vices. With a people who look back to some ancient and indefinite period in their history as an age of glory, an adherence to primitive manners and customs naturally occupies the place of virtue. The stories are generally so constructed as to hold up to admiration a hold and independent spirit of enterprise and adventure. Most of their heroes are drawn from retired or obscure places, and from abject circumstances. Success is seen to crown the efforts of precious boys, orphans, or castaways. But whatever success is had, it is always through the instrumentality of the spirits or Manitoes—the true deities worshipped by all the Algic tribes.

The legend of Manabozho reveals, perhaps, the idea of an incarnation. He is the great spirit-man of northern mythology. The conception of the character reveals rather a monstrosity than a deity, displaying in strong colours far more of the dark and incoherent acts of a spirit of carnality than the benevolent deeds of a god. His birth is shrouded in allegoric mystery. He is made to combine all that is brave, warlike, strong, wise, and great in Indian conception, both of mortal and immortal. He conquers the greatest magician, overcomes fiery serpents, and engages in combats and performs exploits the most extravagant. He has no small share in the Adamic-like labour of naming the animals. He destroys the king of the reptile creation, is drawn into the mouth of a gigantic fish with his canoe, survives a flood by climbing a tree, and recreates the earth from a morsel of ground brought up in the paws of a muskrat. In contrast with these high exploits, he goes about playing low tricks, marries a wife, travels the earth, makes use of low subterfuges, is often in want of food, and, after being tricked and laughed at, is at one time made to covet the ability of a woodpecker, and at another outdone by the simple skill of a child. The great points in which he is exultingly set forth in the story-telling circle, are his great personal strength, readiness of resource, and strong powers of necromancy. Whatever

20

other parts he is made to play, it is the Indian Hercules, Samson, or Proteus that is prominently held up to admiration. It is perhaps natural that rude nations in every part of the world should invent some such mythological existence as the Indian Manabozho, to concentrate their prime exploits upon; for it is the maxim of such nations that "the race is always to the swift, and the battle to the strong."

In closing these remarks, it will not be irrelevant to notice the evidence of the vernacular character and antiquity of the tales, which is furnished by the Pontiac manuscript, preserved in the collections of the Historical Society of Michigan. By this document, which is of the date of 1763, it is shown that this shrewd and talented leader of the Algic tribes, after he had formed the plan of driving the Saxon race from the Continent, appealed to the mythologic belief of the tribes to bring them into his views. It was the Wyandots whom he found it the hardest to convert; and in the general council which he held with the Western chiefs, he narrated before them a tale of a Delaware magician, which is admirably adapted in its incidents to the object he had in view, and affords proof of his foresight and powers of invention. It is deemed of further interest in this connexion, as carrying back the existence of the tales and fables to a period anterior to the final fall of the French power in the Canadas, reaching to within a fraction more than sixty years of their establishment at Detroit. While, however, the authenticity of this curious politico-mythologic tale is undisputed, the names and allusions would show it to be of the modern class of Indian fictions, were not the fact historically known.

H.S.

Wassamo
or the fire plume

Wassamo was living with his parents on the shores of a large bay on the east coast of Lake Michigan. It was at a period when nature spontaneously furnished everything that was wanted, when the Indian used skins for clothing, and flints for arrow heads. It was long before the time that the flag of the white man had been first seen in these lakes, or the sound of an iron axe had been heard. The skill of our people supplied them with weapons to kill game, and instruments to procure bark for their canoes, and to dress and cook their victuals.

One day, when the season had commenced for fish to be plenty near the shore of the lake, Wassamo's mother said to him, "My son, I wish you would go to yonder point, and see if you cannot procure me some fish, and ask your cousin to accompany you." He did so. They set out, and in the course of the afternoon arrived at the fishing ground. His cousin attended to the nets, for he was grown up to manhood, but Wassamo had not quite reached that age. They put their nets in the water and encamped near them, using only a few pieces of birch bark for a lodge to schelter them at night. They lit up a fire, and while they sat conversing with each other, the moon arose. Not a breath of wind disturbed the smooth and bright surface of the lake. Not a cloud was seen. Wassamo looked out on the water toward their nets, and saw that almost all the floats had disappeared. "Cousin", he said, "let us visit our nets, perhaps we are fortunate". They did so, and were rejoiced, as they drew them up, to see the meshes white, here and there, with fish. They landed in fine spirits, and put away their canoe in safety from the winds. "Wassamo", said his cousin, "you cook, that we may eat". He set about it immediately, and soon got his kettle on the fire, while his cousin was lying at his ease on the opposite side of the fire. "Cousin", said Wassamo, "tell me stories, or sing me some love songs". The other obeyed and sung his plaintive songs. He would frequently break off, and tell parts of stories, and then sing again, as suited his feelings or fancy. While thus employed, he unconsciously fell asleep. Wassamo had scarcely noticed it, in his care to watch the kettle, and when the fish were done, he took the kettle off. He spoke to his cousin, but received no answer. He took the wooden ladle and skimmed off the oil, for the fish were very fat. He had a flambeau of twisted bark in one hand to give light, but when he came to take out the fish he did not know how to manage to hold the light. He took off his garters and tied them around his head, and then placed the lighted flambeau above his forehead, so that it was firmly held by the bandage, and threw its light brilliantly around him. Having both hands thus at liberty, he began to take out the fish, every now and then moving his head, as he blew off the oil from the broth. He again spoke to his cousin, but he now perceived by his breathing, that he was asleep. He hastened to finish the removal of the fish, and while he blew over the broth repeatedly, the plume of fire over his forehead waved brilliantly in the air. Suddenly he heard a laugh. There appeared to be one or two persons, at no great distance. "Cousin", he said, to the sleeping boy, "some person is near us. I hear a laugh; awake and let us look out." But his cousin was in a profound sleep. Again he heard the laughing. Looking out as far as the reflection of the fire threw light, he beheld two beautiful young females smiling on him. Their countenances appeared to be perfectly white, and were exceedingly beautiful. He crouched down and pushed his cousin, saying, in a low voice, "awake! awake! here are two young women". But he received no answer. His cousin seemed locked up in one of the deepest slumbers. He started up alone, and went toward the females. He was charmed with their looks, but just as he was about to speak to them, he suddenly feel senseless, and both he and they vanished together.

Some short time afterward the cousin awoke. He saw the kettle near him. Some of the fish were in the bowl. The fire still cast its glare faintly around, but he could discover no person. He waited and waited, but Wassamo did not appear. Perhaps, thought he, he is gone out again to visit the nets. He looked, but the canoe was still in the place where it had been left. He searched and found his footsteps on the ashes. He became uneasy—Netawis! Netawis! (cousin, cousin), he cried out, but there was no answer. He cried out louder and louder, Netawis, Netawis, where are you gone? but still no answer. He started for the edge of the woods, crying Netawis, Netawis. He ran in various directions repeating the same words. The dark woods echoed Netawis, Netawis. He burst into tears and sobbed aloud.

He returned to the fire and sat down, but he had no heart to eat. Various conjectures passed in his mind respecting his cousin. He thought he may have been playing me a trick. No, impossible! or he may have become deranged and ran into the woods. He hoped the morning would bring with it some discovery. But he was oppressed by the thought that the Indians would consider him the murderer of the lost man. "Although", reasoned he, "his parents are my relations, and they know that we are inseparable friends, they will not believe me, if I go home with a report that he is lost. They will say I killed him, and will require blood for blood."

These thoughts weighed upon his mind. He could not sleep. Early in the morning he got up and took in the nets, and set out on foot for the village, running all the way. When they saw him coming, they said, "some accident has happened". When he got in, he told them how his cousin had disappeared. He stated all the circumstances. He kept back nothing. He declared all he knew. Some said, "he has killed him treacherously". Others said, "it is impossible, they were like brothers; sooner than do that they would have given up their lives for each other." He asserted his innocence, and asked them to go and look at the spot of their encampment. Many of the men accordingly went, and found all as he had stated. No footsteps showed that any scuffle had taken place. There were no signs of blood. They came to the conclusion that the young man had got deranged, and strayed away, and was lost. With this belief they returned to the village. But the parents still waited and hoped he would return. Spring came on and the Indians assembled from various quarters. Among them was Wassamo's cousin. He continued to say that he had done nothing to hurt his friends. Anxiety and fear had, however, produced a visible change in his features. He was pale and emaciated. The idea of the blood of his friend and relation being laid to his charge, caused a continual pain of mind.

The parents of Wassamo now demanded the life of Netawis. The village was in an uproar. Some sided with the parents, some with the young man. All showed anxiety in the affair. They at last, however, decided to give the young man's life to the parents. They said they had waited long enough for the return of their son. A day was appointed on which the young man should give his life for his friend's. He still went at large. He said he was not afraid to die, for he had never committed what they laid to his charge. A day or two before the time set to take his life, he wandered in a melancholy mood from the village, following the beach. His feelings were wrought to such a pitch, that he thought once or twice to throw himself into the lake. But he reflected, they will say I was guilty, or I would not have done so. No, I will not, I would prefer dying under their hands." He walked on, thinking of his coming fate, till he reached the sand banks, a short distance from the village. Here we will dismiss him for the present.

When Wassamo fell senseless before the two young women, it must have been some minutes before he recovered, for when he came to himself, he did not know where he was, and had been removed to a distant scene. On recovering his senses he heard persons conversing. One spoke in a tone of authority, saying, "You foolish girls, is this the way you go about at nights, without our knowing it? Put that person you brought on that bed of yours, and let him not lie on the ground." After this Wassamo felt himself moved and placed on a bed. Some time after he opened his eyes fully, and was surprised to find himself in a spacious and superb lodge, extending as far as the eye could reach. One spoke to him, saying, "Stranger, awake, and take something to eat". He arose and sat up. On each side of the lodge he beheld rows of people sitting in regular order. At a distance he could see two prominent persons who looked rather older than the rest, and who appeared to command obedience from all around them. One of them, the Old Spirit man, addressed him. "My son,", said he, "those foolish girls brought you here. They saw you at the fishing ground. When you attempted to approach them, you fell senseless, and they conveyed you underground to this place. But be satisfied. We will make your stay with us pleasant. I am the guardian Spirit of Nagow

Wudjoo. I have wished frequently to get one of your race to intermarry with us. If you can make up your mind to remain, I will give you one of my daughters—the one who brought you away from your parents and friends." The young man dropped his head and made no answer. His silence they construed into an assent to their wishes.

"Your wants", continued the Old Spirit, "will all be supplied, only be careful not to stray away far from this. I am afraid of that Spirit who rules all islands lying in the Lakes. For he demanded my daughter in marriage, and I refused him: when he hears that you are my guest, it may be an inducement for him to harm you. There is my daughter, (he pointed). Take her, she shall be your wife." And forthwith they sat near each other in the lodge, and were considered as married.

"Son-in-law", said the Old Spirit, "I am in want of tobacco. You shall return to visit your parents, and can make known my wishes. For it is very seldom that those few who pass these Sand Hills, offer a piece of tobacco. When they do it, it immediately comes to me. Just so", he added, putting his hand out of the side of the lodge, and drawing in several pieces of tobacco, which some one at that moment happened to offer to the Spirit, for a smooth lake and prosperous voyage. "You see", he said, "every thing offered me on earth, comes immediately to the side of my lodge." Wassamo saw the women also putting their hands to the side of the lodge, and then handing something around, of which all partook. This he found to be offerings of food made by mortals on earth.

"Daughter", said the Old Spirit Woman, Nauonguisk (this is a term applied by women to a son-in-law, etc) cannot eat what we eat, so you can procure him what he is accustomed to. "Yes", she replied, and immediately pushed her hand through the side of the lodge, and took a white fish out of the lake, which she prepared for him. She daily followed the same practice, giving every variety of fish he expressed a wish for. Sometimes it was trout, pike, sturgeon, or any other fish the lake furnished. She did the same with regard to meats, or the flesh of any animal or fowl he asked for. For the animals walked over the roof of the lodge, the birds sat upon its poles, and the waters came so near to its side, that the Spirits had only to extend their hands to the outside to procure whatever they wanted.

One day the Old Spirit said, (although it was perpetual day with them) "son-in-law, you must not be surprised at what you will see, for since you have been with us, you have never seen us go to sleep. It was on account of its being summer, which is constant daylight with us. But now what *you* call winter is approaching. It is six months night with us, you will soon see us lie down, and we shall not get up, but for a moment, throughout the whole winter. Take my advice. Leave not the lodge, but try and amuse yourself. You will find all you wish there", raising his arm slowly and pointing. Wassamo said he would obey, and act as he recommended.

On another occasion a thunder storm came on, when every spirit instantly disappeared. When the storm was over, they all again re-entered the lodge. This scene was repeated during every tempest. "You are surprised", said the Old Spirit", to see us disappear whenever it thunders. The reason is this. A greater Spirit, who lives above, makes those thunders sound and sends his fire. We are afraid, and hide ourselves."

The season of sleep approached, and they, one after another, laid themselves down to their long sleep. In the mean time Wassamo amused himself in the best way he could. His relations got up but once during the whole winter, and they then said it was midnight, and laid down again. "Son-in-law", said the Old Spirit, "you can now, in a few days, start with your wife to visit your relations. You can be absent one year, but after that time you must return. When you get to the village you must first go in alone. Leave your wife a short distance from the lodge, and when you are welcome then send for her. When there, do not be surprised at her disappearance whenever you hear it thunder. You will also prosper in all things, for she is very industrious. All the time that you pass in sleep she will be at work. The distance is short to your village. A road leads directly to it, and when you get there do not forget my wants, as I stated to you before."

Wassamo promised obedience to their directions, and then set out in company with his wife. They travelled in a good road, his wife leading the way, till they got to a rising ground. At the highest point of this, she said, we will soon get to your country. After reaching the summit, they passed, for a short distance, under the lake, and emerged from the water at certain sand banks on the bay of Wekuadong.

Wassamo left his wife concealed in a thicket, while he went toward the village alone. On turning the first point of land, who should he meet but his cousin. "Oh Netawis, Netawis", said his cousin, "you have just come in time to save me. They accuse me of having killed you." Words cannot express their joy. The cousin ran off in haste for the village and entered the lodge where Wassamo's mother was. "Hear me", he said, "I have seen him whom you accuse me of having killed. He will be here in a few moments". The village was in instant commotion. All were anxious to see him whom they had thought dead. While the excitement was at its height Wassamo entered the lodge of his parents. All was joy at the happy meeting. He related all that had happened to him from the moment of his leaving their temporary night lodge with the flame on his head. He told them where he had been, and that he was married. As soon as the excitement of his reception had abated, he told his mother that he had left his wife a short distance from the village. She went immediately in search of her, and soon found her. All the women of the village conducted her to the lodge of her relations. They were astonished at her beauty, at the whiteness of her skin, and more so, at her being able to converse with them in their own language. All was joy in the village ; nothing but feasting could be seen while they had the means of doing so. The Indians came from different quarters, to offer them welcome, and to present their tobacco to the Spirit's daughter.

Thus passed the summer and the fall, and Wassamo's parents and relations, and the Indians around were prospered in all things. But his cousin would never leave him, he was constantly near him, and asking him questions. They took notice that at every thunder storm his wife disappeared, and that at night, as well as during the day, she was never idle. Winter was drawing on, and she told her husband to prepare a lodge for her to pass the season in, and to inform the Indians beforehand of her father's request. He did so, and all now began to move off to their winter quarters. Wassamo also prepared for the season. He gave one half of his lodge to his wife. Before lying down, she said, no one but yourself must pass on the side of the lodge I am on. Winter passed slowly away, and when the sap of the maple began to run, she awoke and commenced her duties as before. She also helped to make sugar. It was never known before or since that so much sugar was made during the season. As soon as the Indians had finished their sugar-making, they left the woods and encamped at their village. They offered tobacco profusely at the lodge of Wassamo, asking for the usual length of life, for success as hunters, and for a plentiful supply of food. Wassamo replied, that he would mention each of their requests to his father-in-law. So much tobacco had been offered, that they were obliged to procure two sacks, made of dressed moose skin, to hold it. On the outside of these skins the different totems of the Indians, who had given the tobacco, were painted and marked, and also those of all persons who had made any request.

When the time arrived for their departure, they told their relatives not to follow them, or see how they disappeared. They then took the two sacks of mooseskin filled with tobacco, and bade adieu to all but Netawis. He insisted on going with them a distance, and when they got to the sand banks he expressed the strongest wish to proceed with them on their journey. Wassamo told him it was impossible, that it was only spirits who could exert the necessary power. They then took an affectionate leave of each other. The young man saw them go into the water and disappear. He returned home and told his friends that he had witnessed their disappearance.

Wassamo and his wife soon reached their home at the grand Sand Hills. The Old Spirit was delighted to see them, and hailed their return with open arms. They presented him with the tobacco, and told him all the requests of the people above. He replied that he would attend to all, but he must first invite his friends to smoke with him. He then sent his Mezhinauwa, to invite his friends the Spirits, and named the time for their reception. Before the time arrived he spoke to his son-in-law. "My son," said he, "some of those Manitoes I have invited are very wicked, and I warn you particularly of the one who wished to marry my daughter. Some of them you will, however, find to be friendly. Take my advice, and when they come in, sit close to your wife—so close you must touch her. If you do not you will be lost, for those who are expected to come in are so powerful, that they will draw you from your seat. You have only to observe my words closely, and all will be well." Wassamo said he would obey.

About midday they commenced coming in. There were spirits from all parts of the country. One entered who smiled on him. He was the guardian Spirit of the Ottowas, and he lived near the present Gitchy Wekuadong (Grand Traverse Bay of Lake Michigan). Soon after, he heard the sounds of the roaring and foaming of waters. Presently they rushed in, and passed through the lodge like a raging tempest. Tremendous pieces of rocks, whole trees, logs, and stumps rolled past, and were borne away by the strong current, with the noise and foaming of some mighty cataract in the spring. It was the guardian spirit of Water-Falls. Again, they heard the roaring of waves, as if beating against a rocky shore. The sounds came rapidly on. In a few moments in rolled the waves of Lake Superior. They were mountain high, and covered with silver-sparkling foam. Wassamo felt their pressure and with difficulty clang to his seat, for they were of frightful appearance, and each one seemed as if it would overwhelm them. This was the last spirit who entered. It was the guardian of Islands in the surrounding lake.

Soon after, the Old Spirit arose and addressed the assembly. "Brothers," he said, "I have invited you to partake with me of the offerings made by the mortals on earth, which have been brought by our relative (pointing to Wassamo). Brothers, you see their wishes and desires, (pointing to the figured mooseskins). Brothers, the offering is worthy of our consideration. Brothers, I see nothing on my part to prevent our granting their requests; they do not appear to be unreasonable. Brothers, the offering is gratifying. Our wants for this article are urgent. Shall we grant their requests? One thing more I would say—Brothers, it is this. There is my son-in-law; he is a mortal. I wish to detain him with me, and it is with us jointly to make him one of us." "Hoke! Hoke!" ran through the whole company of Spirits.

The tobacco was then divided equally among them all. They decided to grant the requests of the people on earth, and also respecting the spirit's son-in-law. When the Spirit of Islands passed Wassamo, he looked angrily at him. The guardian spirit of the Ottowa bands said, "it is very strange that he can never appear anywhere without showing his bad disposition."

When the company was dispersed, the Old Spirit told Wassamo that he should once more visit his parents and relatives, and then it should be only for a short time. "It is merely to go and tell them that their wishes are granted, and then to bid them farewell for ever." Sometime after Wassamo and his wife made this visit. Having delivered his message, he said, "I must now bid you all farewell for ever." His parents and friends raised their voices in loud lamentation. They accompanied him to the Sand Banks, where they all seated themselves to see them make their final departure. The day was mild; the sky clear; not a cloud appeared, nor a breath of wind to disturb the bright surface of the water. The most perfect silence reigned throughout the company. They gazed intently on Wassamo and his wife as they waded out into the water, waving their hands. They saw them go into deeper and deeper water. They saw the waves close over their heads. All at once they raised a loud and piercing wail. They looked again, a red flame, as if the sun had glanced on a billow, marked the spot but the Feather of Flames and his wife had disappeared for ever.

Ojeeg Annung
or the Summer-maker

There lived a celebrated hunter on the southern shores of Lake Superior, who was considered a Manito by some, for there was nothing but what he could accomplish. He lived off the path, in a wild, lonesome place, with a wife whom he loved, and they were blessed with a son, who had attained his thirteenth year. The hunter's name was Ojeeg, or the Fisher, which is the name of an expert, sprightly little animal common to the region. He was so successful in the chase, that he seldom returned without bringing his wife and son a plentiful supply of venison, or other dainties of the woods. and cease crying. He will try to bring summer with all its loveliness. You must then be quiet, and eat that which is set before you."

The squirrel ceased. The boy promised obedience to his advice, and departed. When he reached home, he did as he had been instructed, and all was exactly fulfilled, as it had been predicted by the squirrel.

Ojeeg told him that it was a great undertaking. He must first make a feast, and invite some of his friends to accompany him on a journey. Next day he had a bear roasted whole. All who had been invited to the feast came punctually to the appointment. There were the Otter, Beaver, Lynx, Badger, and Wolverine. After the feast, they arranged it among themselves to set out on the contemplated journey in three days. When the time arrived, the Fisher took leave of his wife and son, as he foresaw that it was for the last time. He and his companions travelled in company day after day, meeting with nothing but the ordinary incidents. On the twentieth day they arrived at the foot of a high mountain, where they saw the tracks of some person who had recently killed an animal, which they knew by the blood that marked the way. The Fisher told his friends that they ought to follow the track, and see if they could not procure something to eat. They followed it for some time; at last they arrived at a lodge, which had been hidden from their view by a hollow in the mountain. Ojeeg told his friends to be very sedate, and not to laugh on any account. The first object that they saw was a man standing at the door of the lodge, but of so deformed a shape that they could not possibly make out who or what sort of a man it could be. His head was enormously large; he had such a queer set of teeth, and no arms. They wondered how he could kill animals. But the secret was soon revealed. He was a great Manito. He invited them to pass the night, to which they consented.

He boiled his meat in a hollow vessel made of wood, and took it out of this singular kettle in some way unknown to his guests. He carefully gave each their portion to eat, but made so many odd movements that the Otter could not refrain from laughing, for he is the only one who is spoken of as a jester. The Manito looked at him with a terrible look, and then made a spring at him, and got on him to smother him, for that was his mode of killing animals. But the Otter, when he felt him on his neck, slipped his head back and made for the door, which he passed in safety; but went out with the curse of the Manito. The others passed the night, and they conversed on different subjects. The Manito told the Fisher that he would accomplish his object, but that it would probably cost him his life. He gave them his advice, directed them how to act, and described a certain road which they must follow, and they would thereby be led to the place of action.

They set off in the morning, and met their friend, the Otter, shivering with cold; but Ojeeg had taken care to bring along some of the meat that had been given him, which he presented to his friend. They pursued their way, and travelled twenty days more before they got to the place which the Manito had told them of. It was a most lofty mountain. They rested on its highest peak to fill their pipes and refresh themselves. Before smoking, they made the customary ceremony, pointing to the heavens, the four winds, the earth, and the zenith; in the mean time, speaking in a loud voice, addressed the Great Spirit, hoping that their object would be accomplished. They then commenced smoking.

They gazed on the sky in silent admiration and astonishment, for they were on so elevated a point, that it appeared to be only a short distance above their heads. After they had finished smoking, they prepared themselves. Ojeeg told the Otter to make the first attempt to try and make a hole in the sky. He consented with a grin. He made a leap, but fell down the hill stunned by the force of his fall; and the snow being moist, and falling on his back, he slid with velocity down the side of the mountain. When he found himself at the bottom, he thought to himself, it is the last time I make such another jump, so I will make the best of my way home. Then it was the turn of the Beaver, who made the attempt, but fell down senseless; then of the Lynx and Badger, who had no better success.

"Now", says the Fisher to the Wolverine, "try your skill; your ancestors were celebrated for their activity, hardihood, and perseverance, and I depend on you for success. Now make the attempt". He did so, but also without success. He leaped the second time, but now they could see that the sky was giving way to their repeated attempts. Mustering strength, he made the third leap, and went in. The Fisher nimbly followed him.

They found themselves in a beautiful plain, extending as far as the eye could reach, covered with flowers of a thousand different hues and fragrance. Here and there were clusters of tall, shady trees, separated by innumerable streams of the purest water, which wound around their courses under the cooling shades, and filled the plain with countless beautiful lakes, whose banks and bosom were covered with water-fowl, basking and sporting in the sun. The trees were alive with birds of different plumage, warbling their sweet notes, and delighted with perpetual spring.

The Fisher and his friend beheld very long lodges, and the celestial inhabitants amusing themselves at a distance. Words cannot express the beauty and charms of the place. The lodges were empty of inhabitants, but they saw them lined with mocuks (baskets) of different sizes, filled with birds and fowls of different plumage. Ojeeg thought of his son, and immediately commenced cutting open the mocuks and letting out the birds, who descended in whole flocks through the opening which they had made. The warm air of those regions also rushed down through the opening, and spread its genial influence over the north.

When the celestial inhabitants saw the birds let loose, and the warm gales descending, they raised a shout like thunder, and ran for their lodges. But it was too late. Spring, summer, and autumn had gone; even perpetual summer had almost all gone; but they separated it with a blow, and only a part descended; but the ends were so mangled, that, wherever it prevails among the lower inhabitants, it is always sickly.

When the Wolverine heard the noise, he made for the opening and safely descended. Not so the Fisher. Anxious to fulfil his son's wishes, he continued to break open the mocuks. He was, at last, obliged to run also, but the opening was now closed by the inhabitants. He ran with all his might over the plains of heaven, and, it would appear, took a northerly direction. He saw his pursuers so close that he had to climb the first large tree he came to. They commenced shooting at him with their arrows, but without effect, for all his body was invulnerable except the space of about an inch near the tip of his tail. At last one of the arrows hit the spot, for he had in this chase assumed the shape of the Fisher after whom he was named.

He looked down from the tree, and saw some among his assailants with the totems of his ancestors. He claimed relationship, and told them to desist, which they only did at the approach of night. He then came down to try and find an opening in the celestial plain, by which he might descend to the earth. But he could find none. At last, becoming faint from the loss of blood from the wound on his tail, he laid himself down towards the north of the plain, and, stretching out his limbs, said, "I have fulfilled my promise to my son, though it has cost me my life; but I die satisfied in the idea that I have done so much good, not only for him, but for my fellow-beings. Hereafter I will be a sign to the inhabitants below for ages to come, who will venerate my name for having succeeded in procuring the varying seasons. They will now have from eight to ten moons without snow."

He was found dead next morning, but they left him as they found him, with the arrow sticking in his tail, as it can be plainly seen, at this time, in the heavens.

The celestial sisters

Waupee, or the White Hawk, lived in a remote part of the forest, where animals and birds were abundant. Every day he returned from the chase with the reward of his toil, for he was one of the most skilful and celebrated hunters of his tribe. With a tall, manly form, and the fire of youth beaming from his eye, there was no forest too gloomy for him to penetrate, and no track made by the numerous kinds of birds and beasts which he could not follow.

One day he penetrated beyond any point which he had before visited. He travelled through an open forest, which enabled him to see a great distance. At length he beheld a light breaking through the foliage, which made him sure that he was on the borders of a prairie. It was a wide plain covered with grass and flowers. After walking some time without a path, he suddenly came to a ring worn through the sod, as if it had been made by footsteps following a circle. But what excited his surprise was, that there was no path leading to or from it. Not the least trace of footsteps could be found, even in a crushed leaf or broken twig. He thought he would hide himself, and lie in wait to see what this circle meant. Presently he heard the faint sounds of music in the air. He looked up in the direction they came from, and saw a small object descending from above. At first it looked like a mere speck, but rapidly increased, and, as it came down, the music became plainer and sweeter. It assumed the form of a basket, and was filled with twelve sisters of the most lovely forms and enchanting beauty. As soon as the basket touched the ground, they leaped out, and began to dance round the magic ring, striking, as they did so, a shining ball as we strike the drum. Waupee gazed upon their graceful forms and motions from his place of concealment. He admired them all, but was most pleased with the youngest. Unable longer to restrain his admiration, he rushed out and endeavoured to seize her. But the sisters, with the quickness of birds, the moment they descried the form of a man, leaped back into the basket and were drawn up into the sky.

Regretting his ill luck and indiscretion, he gazed till he saw them disappear, and then said, "They are gone, and I shall see them no more." He returned to his solitary lodge, but found no relief to his mind. Next day he went back to the prairie, and took his station near the ring; but in order to deceive the sisters, he assumed the form of an opossum. He had not waited long, when he saw the wicker car descend, and heard the same sweet music. They commenced the same sportive dance, and seemed even more beautiful and graceful than before. He crept slowly towards the ring, but the instant the sisters saw him they were startled, and sprang into their car. It rose but a short distance, when one of the elder sisters spoke. "Perhaps," said she, "it is come to show us how the game is played by mortals." "Oh no!" the youngest replied; "quick, let us ascend." And all joining in a chant, they rose out of sight.

The White Hawk returned to his own form again, and walked sorrowfully back to his lodge. But the night seemed a very long one, and he went back betimes the next day. He reflected upon the sort of plan to follow to secure success. He found an old stump near by, in which there were a number of mice. He thought their small form would not create alarm, and accordingly assumed it. He brought the stump and sat it up near the ring. The sisters came down and resumed their sport. "But see," cried the younger sister, "that stump was not there before." She ran affrighted towards the car. They only smiled, and gathering round the stump, struck it in jest, when out ran the mice, and Waupee among the rest. They killed them all but one, which was pursued by the youngest sister; but just as she had raised her stick to kill it, the form of White Hawk arose, and he clasped his prize in his arms. The other eleven sprang to their basket and were drawn up to the skies.

Waupee exerted all his skill to please his bride and win her affections. He wiped the tears from her eyes. He related his adventures in the chase. He dwelt upon the charms of life on the earth. He was incessant in his attentions, and picked out the way for her to walk as he led her gently towards his lodge. He felt his heart glow with joy as she entered, it, and from that moment he was one of the happiest of men. Winter and summer passed rapidly away, and their happiness was increased by the addition of a beautiful boy to their lodge. Waupee's wife was a daughter of one of the stars, and as the scenes of earth began to pall upon her sight, she sighed to revisit her father. But she was obliged to hide these feelings from her husband. She remembered the charm that would carry her up, and took occasion, while the White Hawk was engaged in the chase, to construct a wicker basket, which she kept concealed. In the mean time she collected such rarities from the earth as she thought would please her father, as well as the most dainty kinds of food. When all was in readiness, she went out one day, while Waupee was absent, to the charmed ring, taking her little son with her. As soon as they got into the car, she commenced her song and the basket rose. As the song was wafted by the wind, it caught her husband's ear. It was a voice which he well knew, and he instantly ran to the prairie. But he could not reach the ring before he saw his wife and child ascend. He lifted up his voice in loud appeals, but they were unavailing. The basket still went up. He watched it till it became a small speck, and finally it vanished in the sky. He then bent his head down to the ground, and was miserable.

Waupee bewailed his loss through a long winter and a long summer. But he found no relief. He mourned his wife's loss sorely, but his son's still more. In the mean time his wife had reached her home in the stars, and almost forgot, in the blissful employments there, that she had left a husband on the earth. She was reminded of this by the presence of her son, who, as he grew up, became anxious to visit the scene of his birth. His grandfather said to his daughter one day, "Go, my child, and take your son down to his father, and ask him to come up and live with us. But tell him to bring along a specimen of each kind of bird and animal he kills in the chase." She accordingly took the boy and descended. The White Hawk, who was ever near the enchanted spot, heard her voice as she came down the sky. His heart beat with impatience as he saw her form and that of his son, and they were soon clasped in his arms.

He heard the message of the Star, and began to hunt with the greatest activity, that he might collect the present. He spent whole nights, as well as days, in searching for every curious and beautiful bird or animal. He only preserved a tail, foot, or wing of each, to identify the species; and, when all was ready, they went to the circle and were carried up.

Great joy was manifested on their arrival at the starry plains. The Star Chief invited all his people to a feast, and, when they had assembled, he proclaimed aloud, that each one might take of the earthly gifts such as he liked best. A very strange confusion immediately arose. Some chose a foot, some a wing, some a tail, and some a claw. Those who selected tails or claws were changed into animals, and ran off; the others assumed the form of birds, and flew away. Waupee chose a white hawk's feather. His wife and son followed his example, when each one became a white hawk. He spread his wings, and, followed by his wife and son, descended with the other birds to the earth, where his species are still to be found.

Tau Wau Chee Hezkaw or the White Feather

There was an old man living in the centre of a forest, with his grandson, whom he had taken when quite an infant. The child had no parents, brothers, or sisters; they had all been destroyed by six large giants, and he had been informed that he had no other relative living besides his grandfather. The band to whom he belonged had put up their children on a wager in a race against those of the giants, and had thus lost them. There was an old tradition in the band, that it would produce a great man, who would wear a white feather, and who would astonish every one with his skill and feats of bravery.

The grandfather, as soon as the child could play about, gave him a bow and arrows to amuse himself. He went into the edge of the woods one day, and saw a rabbit; but, not knowing what it was, he ran home and described it to his grandfather. He told him what it was, that its flesh was good to eat, and that, if he would shoot one of his arrows into its body, he would kill it. He did so, and brought the little animal home, which he asked his grandfather to boil, that they might feast on it. He humoured the boy in this, and encouraged him to go on in acquiring the knowledge of hunting, until he could kill deer and larger animals; and he became, as he grew up, an expert hunter. As they lived alone, and away from other Indians, his curiosity was excited to know what was passing in the world. One day he came to the edge of a prairie, where he saw ashes like those at his grandfather's lodge, and lodge-poles left standing. He returned and inquired whether his grandfather had put up the poles and made the fire. He was answered no, nor did he believe that he had seen anything of the kind. It was all imagination.

Another day he went out to see what there was curious; and, on entering the woods, he heard a voice calling out to him, "Come here, you destined wearer of the White Feather. You do not yet wear it, but you are worthy of it. Return home and take a short nap. You will dream of hearing a voice, which will tell you to rise and smoke. You will see in your dream a pipe, smoking-sack, and a large white feather. When you awake you will find these articles. Put the feather on your head, and you will become a great hunter, a great warrior, and a great man, capable of doing anything. As a proof that you will become a great hunter, when you smoke the smoke will turn into pigeons." The voice then informed him who he was, and disclosed the true character of his grandfather, who had imposed upon him. The voice-spirit then gave him a *vine*, and told him he was of an age to revenge the injuries of his relations. "When you meet your enemy," continued the spirit, "you will run a race with him. He will not see the vine, because it is enchanted. While you are running, you will throw it over his head and entangle him, so that you will win the race."

Long ere this speech was ended he had turned to the quarter from which the voice proceeded, and was astonished to behold a man, for as yet he had never seen any man besides his grandfather, whose object it was to keep him in ignorance. But the circumstance that gave him the most surprise was, that this man, who had the looks of great age, was composed of *wood* from his breast downward, and appeared to be fixed in the earth.

He returned home, slept, heard the voice, awoke, and found the promised articles. His grandfather was greatly surprised to find him with a white feather on his forehead, and to see flocks of pigeons flying out of his lodge. He then recollected what had been predicted, and began to weep at the prospect of losing his charge.

Invested with these honours, the young man departed the next morning to seek his enemies and gratify his revenge. The giants lived in a very high lodge in the middle of a wood. He travelled on till he came to this lodge, where he found that his coming had been made known by *the little spirits who carry the news.* The giants came out, and gave a cry of joy as they saw him coming. When he approached nearer, they began to make sport of him, saying, "Here comes the little man with the white feather, who is to achieve such wonders." They, however, spoke very fair to him, when he came up, saying he was a brave man, and would do brave things. This they said to encourage, and the more surely to deceive him. He, however, understood the object.

He went fearlessly up to the lodge. They told him to commence the race with the smallest of their number. The point to which they were to run was a peeled tree towards the rising sun, and then back to the starting-place, which was marked by a Chaunkahpee, or war-club, made of iron. This club was the stake, and whoever won it was to use in in beating the other's brains out. If he beat the first giant, he was to try the second, and so on until they had all measured speed with him. He won the first race by a dexterous use of the vine, and immediately despatched his competitor, and cut off his head. Next morning he ran with the second giant, whom he also outran, killed, and decapitated. He proceeded in this way for five successive mornings, always conquering by the use of his vine, and cutting off the heads of the vanquished. The survivers acknowledged his power, but prepared secretly to deceive him. They wished him to leave the heads he had cut off, as they believed they could again reunite them with the bodies, by means of one of their *medicines.* White Feather insisted, however, in carrying all the heads to his grandfather. One more contest was to be tried, which would decide the victory; but, before going to the giant's lodge on the sixth morning, he met his old counsellor in the woods, who was stationary. He told him that he was about to be deceived. That he had never known any other sex but his own; but that, as he went on his way to the lodge, he would meet the most beautiful woman in the world. He must pay no attention to her, but, on meeting her, he must wish himself changed into a make elk. The transformation would take place immediately, when he must go to feeding and not regard her.

He proceeded towards the lodge, met the female, and became an elk. She reproached him for having turned himself into an elk on seeing her; said she had travelled a great distance for the purpose of seeing him, and becoming his wife. Now this woman was the sixth giant, who had assumed this disguise; but Tau-Wau-Chee-Hezkaw remained in ignorance of it. Her reproaches and her beauty affected him so much, that he wished himself a man again, and he at

45

once resumed his natural shape. They sat down together, and he began to caress her, and make love to her. He finally ventured to lay his head on her lap and went to sleep. She pushed his head aside at first, for the purpose of trying if he was really asleep; and when she was satisfied he was, she took her axe and broke his back. She then assumed her natural shape, which was in the form of the sixth giant, and afterward changed him into a dog, in which degraded form he followed his enemy to the lodge. He took the white feather from his brow, and wore it as a trophy on his own head.

There was an Indian village at some distance, in which there lived two girls, who were rival sisters, the daughters of a chief. They were fasting to acquire power for the purpose of enticing the wearer of the white feather to visit their village. They each secretly hoped to engage his affections. Each one built herself a lodge at a short distance from the village. The giant, knowing this, and having now obtained the valued plume, went immediately to visit them. As he approached, the girls saw and recognised the feather. The eldest sister prepared her lodge with great care and parade, so as to attract the eye. The younger, supposing that he was a man of sense, and would not be enticed by mere parade, touched nothing in her lodge, but left it as it ordinarily was. The eldest went out to meet him, and invited him in. He accepted her invitation, and made her his wife. The younger invited the enchanted dog into her lodge, and made him a good bed, and treated him with as much attention as if he were her husband.

The giant, supposing that whoever possessed the white feather possessed also all its virtues, went out upon the prairie to hunt, but returned unsuccessful. The dog went out the same day a hunting upon the banks of a river. He drew a stone out of the water, which immediately became a beaver. The next day the giant followed the dog, and, hiding behind a tree, saw the manner in which the dog went into the river and drew out a stone, which at once turned into a beaver. As soon as the dog left the place, the giant went to the river, and observing the same manner, drew out a stone, and had the satisfaction of seeing it transformed into a beaver. Tying it to his belt, he carried it home, and as is customary, threw it down at the door of the lodge before he entered. After being seated a short time, he told his wife to bring in his belt or hunting girdle. She did so, and returned with it, with nothing tied to it but a *stone*.

The next day, the dog, finding his method of catching beavers had been discovered, went to a wood at some distance, and broke off a charred limb from

47

a burned tree, which instantly became a bear. The giant, who had again watched him, did the same, and carried a bear home; but his wife, when she came to go out for it, found nothing but a black stick tied to his belt.

The giant's wife determined she would go to her father, and tell him what a valuable husband she had, who furnished her lodge with abundance. She set out while her husband went to hunt. As soon as they had departed, the dog made signs to his mistress to sweat him after the manner of the Indians. She accordingly made a lodge just large enough for him to creep in. She then put in heated stones, and poured on water. After this had been continued the usual time, he came out a very handsome young man, but had not the power of speech.

Meantime the elder daughter had reached her father's, and, told him of the manner in which her sister supported a dog, treating him as her husband, and of the singular skill this animal had in hunting. The old man, suspecting there was some magic in it, sent a deputation of young men and women to ask her to come to him, and bring her dog along. When this deputation arrived, they were surprised to find, in the place of the dog, so fine a young man. They both accompanied the messengers to the father, who was no less astonished. He assembled all the old and wise men of the nation to see the exploits which, it was reported, the young man could perform. The giant was among the number. He took his pipe and filled it, and passed it to the Indians, to see if anything would happen when they smoked. It was passed around to the dog, who made a sign to hand it to the giant first, which was done, but nothing effected. He then took it himself. He made a sign to them to put the white feather upon his head. This was done, and immediately he regained his speech. He then commenced smoking, and behold! immense flocks of white and blue pigeons rushed from the smoke.

The chief demanded of him his history, which he faithfully recounted. When it was finished, the chief ordered that the giant should be transformed into a dog, and turned into the middle of the village, where the boys should pelt him to death with clubs. This sentence was executed.

The chief then ordered, on the request of the White Feather, that all the young men should employ themselves four days in making arrows. He also asked for a buffalo robe. This robe he cut into thin shreds, and sowed in the prairie. At the end of the four days he invited them to gather together all their arrows, and accompany him to a buffalo hunt. They found that these shreds of

skin had grown into a very large herd of buffalo. They killed as many as they pleased, and enjoyed a grand festival, in honour of his triumph over the Giants.

Having accomplished their labour, the White Feather got his wife to ask her father's permission to go with him on a visit to his grandfather. He replied to this solicitation, that a woman must follow her husband into whatever quarter of the world he may choose to go.

The young man then placed the white feather in his frontlet, and, taking his war-club in his hand, led the way into the forest, followed by his faithful wife.

Peboan and Seegwun

An old man was sitting alone in his lodge, by the side of a frozen stream. It was the close of winter, and his fire was almost out. He appeared very old and very desolate. His locks were white with age, and he trembled in every joint. Day after day passed in solitude, and he heard nothing but the sounds of the tempest, sweeping before it the new-fallen snow.

One day, as his fire was just dying, a handsome young man approached and entered his dwelling. His cheeks were red with the blood of youth, his eyes sparkled with animation, and a smile played upon his lips. He walked with a light and quick step. His forehead was bound with a wreath of sweet grass, in place of a warrior's frontlet, and he carried a bunch of flowers in his hand.

"Ah, my son", said the old man, "I am happy to see you. Come in. Come, tell me of your adventures, and what strange lands you have been to see. Let us pass the night together. I will tell you of my prowess and exploits, and what I can perform. You shall do the same, and we will amuse ourselves."

He then drew from his sack a curiously-wrought antique pipe, and having filled it with tobacco, rendered mild by an admixture of certain leaves, handed it to his guest. When this ceremony was concluded they began to speak.

"I blow my breath", said the old man, "and the streams stand still. The water becomes stiff and hard as clear stone."

"I breathe", said the young man, "and flowers spring up all over the plains".

"I shake my locks", retorted the old man, "and snow covers the land. The leaves fall from the trees at my command, and my breath blows them away. The birds get up from the water, and fly to a distant land. The animals hide themselves from my breath, and the very ground becomes as hard as flint."

"I shake my ringlets", rejoined the young man, "and warm showers of soft rain fall upon the earth. The plants lift up their heads out of the earth, like the eyes of children glistening with delight. My voice recalls the birds. The warmth of my breath unlocks the streams. Music fills the groves wherever I walk, and all nature rejoices."

At length the sun began to rise. A gentle warmth came over the place. The tongue of the old man became silent. The robin and bluebird began to sing on the top of the lodge. The stream began to murmur by the door, and the fragrance of growing herbs and flowers came softly on the vernal breeze.

Daylight fully revealed to the young man the character of his entertainer. When he looked upon him, he had the icy visage of Peboan (Winter). Streams began to flow from his eyes. As the sun increased, he grew less and less in stature, and anon had melted completely away. Nothing remained on the place of his lodge fire but the miskodeed, the Claytonia Virginica, a small white flower, with a pink border, which is one of the earliest species of Northern plants.

Mon-Daw-Min or the origin of indian corn

In times past, a poor Indian was living with his wife and children in a beautiful part of the country. He was not only poor, but inexpert in procuring food for his family, and his children were all too young to give him assistance. Although poor, he was a man of a kind and contented disposition. He was always thankful to the Great Spirit for everything he received. The same disposition was inherited by his eldest son, who had now arrived at the proper age to undertake the ceremony of the Ke-ig-uish-im-o-win, or fast, to see what kind of a spirit would be his guide and guardian through life. Wunzh, for this was his name, had been an obedient boy from his infancy, and was of a pensive, thoughtful, and mild disposition, so that he was beloved by the whole family. As soon as the first indications of spring appeared, they built him the customary little lodge, at a retired spot some distance from their own, where he would not be disturbed during this solemn rite. In the mean time he prepared himself, and immediately went into it and commenced his fast. The first few days he amused himself in the mornings by walking in the woods and over the mountains, examining the early plants and flowers, and in this way prepared

53

himself to enjoy his sleep, and, at the same time, stored his mind with pleasant ideas for his dreams. While he rambled through the woods, he felt a strong desire to know how the plants, herbs, and berries grew, without any aid from man, and why it was that some species were good to eat, and others possessed medicinal or poisonous juices. He recalled these thoughts to mind after he became too languid to walk about, and had confined himself strictly to the logde; he wished he could dream of something that would prove a benefit to his father and family, and to all others. "True!" he thought, "the Great Spirit made all things, and it is to him that we owe our lives. But could he not make it easier for us to get our food, than by hunting animals and taking fish? I must try to find out this in my visions."

On the third day he became weak and faint, and kept his bed. He fancied, while thus lying, that he saw a handsome young man coming down from the sky and advancing towards him. He was richly and gayly dressed, having on a great many garments of green and yellow colours, but differing in their deeper or lighter shades. He had a plume of waving feathers on his head, and all his motions were graceful.

"I am sent to you, my friend", said the celestial visiter, "by that Great Spirit who made all things in the sky and on the earth. He has seen and knows your motives in fasting. He sees that it is from a kind and benevolent wish to do good to your people, and to procure a benefit for them, and that you do not seek for strength in war or the praise of warriors. I am sent to instruct you, and show you how you can do your kindred good." He then told the young man to arise, and prepare to wrestle with him, as it was only by this means that he could hope to succeed in his wishes. Wunzh knew he was weak from fasting, but he felt his courage rising in his heart, and immediately got up, determined to die rather than fail. He commenced the trial, and, after a protracted effort, was almost exhausted, when the beautiful stranger said, "My friend, it is enough for once; I will come again to try you;" and, smiling on him, he ascended in the air in the same direction from which he came. The next day the celestial visiter reappeared at the same hour and renewed the trial. Wunzh felt that his strength was even less than the day before, but the courage of his mind seemed to increase in proportion as his body became weaker. Seeing this, the stranger again spoke to him in the same words he used before, adding, "To-morrow will be your last trial. Be strong, my friend, for this is the only way you can overcome me, and obtain the boon you seek". On the

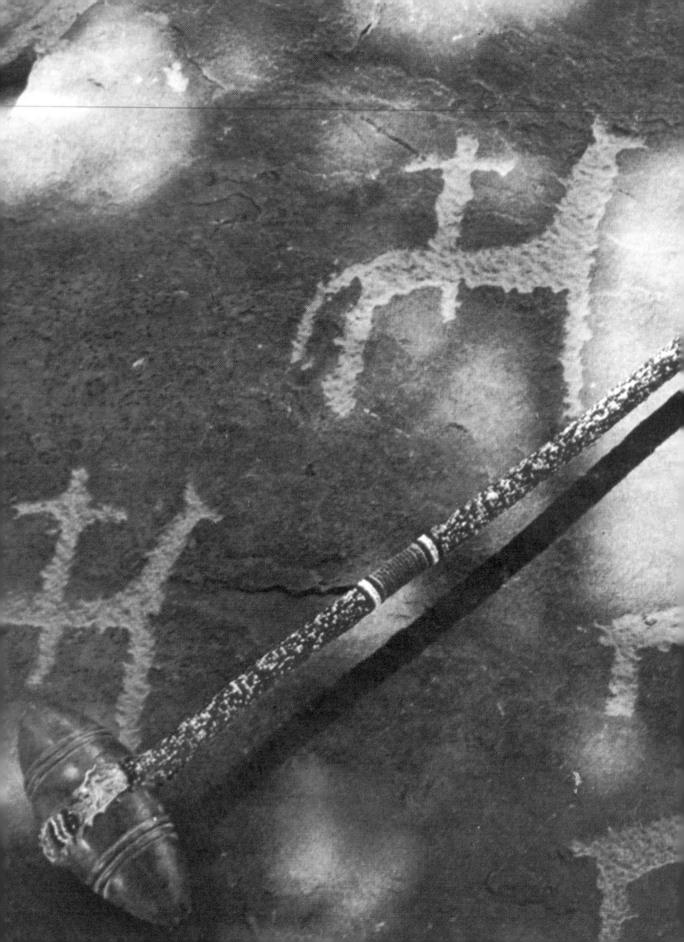

third day he again appeared at the same time and renewed the struggle. The poor youth was very faint in body, but grew stronger in mind at every contest, and was determined to prevail or perish in the attempt. He exerted his utmost powers, and after the contest had been continued the usual time, the stranger ceased his efforts and declared himself conquered. For the first time he entered the lodge, and sitting down beside the youth, he began to deliver his instructions to him, telling him in what manner he should proceed to take advantage of his victory.

"You have won your desires of the Great Spirit", said the stranger. "You have wrestled manfully. To-morrow will be the seventh day of your fasting. Your father will give you food to strengthen you, and as it is the last day of trial, you will prevail. I know this, and now tell you what you must do to benefit your family and your tribe. To-morrow", he repeated, "I shall meet you and wrestle with you for the last time; and, as soon as you have prevailed against me, you will strip off my garments and throw me down, clean the earth of roots and weeds, make it soft, and bury me in the spot. When you have done this, leave my body in the earth, and do not disturb it, but come occasionally to visit the place, to see whether I have come to life, and be careful never to let the grass or weeds grow on my grave. Once a month cover me with fresh earth. If you follow my instructions, you will accomplish your object of doing good to your fellow-creatures by teaching them the knowledge I now teach you." He then shook him by the hand and disappeared.

In the morning the youth's father came with some slight refreshments, saying, "My son, you have fasted long enough. If the Great Spirit will favour you, he will do it now. It is seven days since you have tasted food, and you must not sacrifice your life. The Master of Life does not require that." "My father", replied the youth, "wait till the sun goes down. I have a particular reason for extending my fast to that hour." "Very well", said the old man, "I shall wait till the hour arrives, and you feel inclined to eat".

At the usual hour of the day the sky-visiter returned, and the trial of strength was renewed. Although the youth had not availed himself of his father's offer of food, he felt that new strength had been given to him, and that exertion had renewed his strength and fortified his courage. He grasped his angelic antagonist with supernatural strength, threw him down, took from him his beautiful garments and plume, and finding him dead, immediately buried him on the spot, taking all the precautions he had been told of, and being very confident, at the same time, that his friend would again come to life. He then returned to his father's lodge, and partook sparingly of the meal that had been prepared for him. But he never for a moment forgot the grave of his friend. He carefully visited is throughout the spring, and weeded out the grass, and kept the ground in a soft and pliant state. Very soon he saw the tops of the green plumes coming through the ground; and the more careful he was to obey his instructions in keeping the ground in order, the faster they grew. He was, however, careful to conceal the exploit from his father. Days and weeks had passed in this way. The summer was now drawing towards a close, when one day, after a long absence in hunting, Wunzh invited his father to follow him to the quiet and lonesome spot of his former fast. The lodge had been removed, and the weeks kept from growing on the circle where it stood, but in its place stood a tall and graceful plant, with bright-coloured silken hair, surmounted with nodding plumes and stately leaves, and golden clusters on each side. "It is my friend", shouted the lad; "it is the friend of all mankind. It is *Mondawmin.* (The Alfic name for corn. The word is manifestly a trinary compound from *monedo,* spirit; *min,* a grain or berry; and *iaw,* the verb substantive.) We need no longer rely on hunting alone; for, as long as this gift is cherished and taken care of, the ground itself will give us a living." He then pulled an ear. "See, my father", said he, "this is what I fasted for. The Great Spirit has listened to my voice, and sent us something new, and henceforth our people will not alone depend upon the chase or upon the waters."

He then communicated to his father the instructions given him by the stranger. He told him that the broad husks must be torn away, as he had pulled off the garments in his wrestling; and having done this, directed him how the ear must be held before the fire till the outer skin became brown, while all the milk was retained in the grain. The whole family then united in a feast on the newly-grown ears, expressing gratitude to the Merciful Spirit who gave it. So corn came in to the world, and has ever since been preserved.

Manabozho or the great incarnation of the north

Manabozho was living with his grandmother near the edge of a wide prairie. On this prairie he first saw animals and birds of every kind. He there also saw exhibitions of divine power in the sweeping tempests, in the thunder and lightning, and the various shades of light and darkness, which form a never-ending scene of observation. Every new sight he beheld in the heavens was a subject of remark; every new animal or bird an object of deep interest; and every sound uttered by the animal creation a new lesson, which he was expected to learn. He often trembled at what he heard and saw. To this scene his grand-mother sent him at an early age to watch. The first sound he heard was that of the owl, at which he was greatly terrified, and, quickly descending the tree he had climbed, he ran with alarm to the lodge. "Noko! Noko!" (An abbreviated term for "my grandmother," derived from *no-kó-miss*) he cried, "I have heard a monedo". She laughed at his fears, and asked him what kind of a noise it made. He answered, "It makes a noise like this: Ko-ko-ko-ho." She told him that he was young and foolish; that what he had heard was only a bird, deriving its name from the noise it made.

He went back and continued his watch. While there, he thought to himself, "It is singular that I am so simple, and my grandmother so wise, and that I have neither father nor mother. I have never heard a word about them. I must ask and find out." He went home and sat down silent and dejected. At length his grandmother asked him, "Manabozho, what is the matter with you?" He answered, "I wish you would tell me whether I have any parents living, and who my relatives are." Knowing that he was of a wicked and revengeful disposition, she dreaded telling him the story of his parentage, but he insisted on her compliance. "Yes," she said, "you have a father and three brothers living. Your mother is dead. She was taken without the consent of her parents by your father the West. Your brothers are the North, East, and South, and, being older than yourself, your father has given them great power with the winds, according to their names. You are the youngest of his children. I have nourished you from your infancy, for your mother died in giving you birth, owing to the ill treatment of your father. I have no relations besides you this side of the planet in which I was born, and from which I was precipitated by female jealousy. Your mother was my only child, and you are my only hope."

He appeared to be rejoiced to hear that his father was living, for he had already thought in his heart to try and kill him. He told his grandmother he should set out in the morning to visit him. She said it was a long distance to the place where Ningabiun (the west wind) lived. But that had no effect to stop him, for he had now attained manhood, possessed a giant's height, and was endowed by nature with a giant's strength and power. He set out and soon reached the place, for every step he took covered a large surface of ground. The meeting took place on a high mountain in the West. His father was very happy to see him. He also appeared pleased. They spent some days in talking with each other. One evening Manabozho asked his father what he was most afraid of on earth. He replied, "Nothing." "But is there not something you dread here? tell me." At last his father said, yielding, "Yes, there is a black stone found in such a place. It is the only thing earthly I am afraid of; for if it should hit me or any part of my body, it would injure me very much." He said this as a secret, and in return asked his son the same question. Knowing each other's power, although the son's was limited, the father feared him on account of his great strength. Manabozho answered, "Nothing!" intending to avoid the question, or to refer to some harmless object as the one of which he was afraid. He was asked again and again, and answered "Nothing!" But the West said, "There must be something you are afraid of." "Well' I will tell you," says Manabozho, "what it is." But, before he would pronounce the word, he affected great dread. "*Ie-ee-Ie-ee—* it is—it is," said he, "yeo! I cannot name it, I am seized with a dread." The West told him to banish his fears. He commenced again, in a strain of mock sensitiveness repeating the same words; at last he cried out. "It is the root of the *apukuwa.*" He appeared to be exhausted by the effort of pronouncing the word, in all this skilfully acting a studied part.

Some time after he observed, "I will get some of the black rock." The West said, "Far be it from you; do not do so, my son." He still persisted. "Well," said the father, "I will also get the apukwa root." Manabozho immediately cried out, "*Kago! kago!*" (Do not—Do not) affecting, as before, to be in great dread of it, but really wishing, by this course, to urge on the West to procure it, that he might draw him into combat. He went out and got a large piece of the black rock, and brought it home. The West also took care to bring the dreaded root.

In the course of conversation he asked his father whether he had been the cause of his mother's death. The answer was "Yes!" He then took up the rock. and struck him. Blow led to blow, and here commenced an obstinate and furious combat, which continued several days. Fragments of the rock, broken off under Manabozho's blows, can be seen in various places to this day. The root did not prove as mortal a weapon as his well-acted fears had led his father to expect, although he suffered severely from the blows. This battle commenced on the mountains. The West was forced to give ground. Manabozho drove him across rivers, and over mountains and lakes, and at last he came to the brink of this world.

"Hold!" cried he, "my son, you know my power, and that it is impossible to kill me. Desist, and I will also portion you out with as much power as your brothers. The four quarters of the globe are already occupied; but you can go and do a great deal of good to the people of this earth, which is infested with large serpents, beasts, and monsters, who make great havoc among the inhabitants. Go and do good. You have the power now to do so, and your fame with the beings of this earth will last for ever. When you have finished your work, I will have a place provided for you. You will then go and sit with your brother Kabibboonocca in the north."

Manabozho was pacified. He returned to his lodge, where he was confined by the wounds he had received. But from his grandmother's skill in medicines he was soon recovered. She told him that his grandfather, who had come to the earth in search of her, had been killed by Megissogwon, who lived on the opposite side of the great lake.

Iena or
the Magic Bundle

There was once a poor man called Iena, who was in the habit of wandering about from place to place, forlorn, without relations and almost helpless. One day, as he went on a hunting excursion, he hung up his bundle on the branch of a tree, to relieve himself from the burden of carrying it, and then went in quest of game. On returning to the spot in the evening, he was surprised to find a small but neat lodge built in the place where he had left his bundle; and on looking in, he beheld a beautiful female sitting in the lodge, with his blanket lying beside her. During the day he had been fortunate in killing a deer, which he laid down at the lodge door. But, to his surprise, the woman, in her attempt to bring it in, broke both her legs. He looked at her with astonishment, and thought to himself, "I supposed I was blessed, but I find my mistake. Gweengweesheee", (the night-hawk) said he, "I will leave my game with you, that you may feast on it".

He then took up his bundle and departed. After walking some time he came to another tree, on which he suspended his bundle as before, and went in search of game. Success again rewarded his efforts, and he returned bringing a deer, but found, as before, that a lodge had sprung up in the place where he had suspended his bundle. He looked in, and saw, as before, a beautiful female sitting alone, with his bundle by her side. She arose, and came out to bring in the deer, which he had deposited at the door, and he immediately went into the lodge and sat by the fire, as he felt fatigued with the day's labours. Wondering, at last, at the delay of the woman, he arose, and peeping through the door of the lodge, beheld her eating all the fat of the deer. He exclaimed, "I thought I was blessed, but I find I am mistaken". Then addressing the woman, "Poor Wabizhas", said he, "feast on the game that I have brought". He again took up his bundle and departed, and, as usual, hung it up on the branch of a tree, and wandered off in quest of game. In the evening he returned with his customary good luck, bringing in a fine deer, and again found a lodge occupying the place of his bundle. He gazed through an aperture in the side of the lodge, and saw a beautiful woman sitting alone, with a bundle by her side. As soon as he entered the lodge, she arose with alacrity, brought in the carcass, cut it up, and hung up the meat to dry. After this, she prepared a portion of it for the supper of the weary hunter. The man thought to himself, "Now I am certainly blessed". He continued his practice of hunting every day, and the woman, on his return, always readily took care of the meat, and prepared his meals for him. One thing, however, astonished him; he had never, as yet, seen her eat anything, and kindly said to her, "Why do you not eat?" She replied, "I have food of my own, which I eat".

On the fourth day he brought home with him a branch of uzadi as a cane, which he placed, with his game, at the door of the lodge. His wife, as usual, went out to prepare and bring in the meat. While thus engaged, he heard her laughing to herself, and saying, "This is very acceptable". The man, in peeping out to see the cause of her joy, saw her, with astonishment, eating the bark of the poplar cane in the same manner that beavers gnaw. He then exclaimed, "Ho, ho! Ho, ho! this is Amik;" (the beaver) and ever afterward he was careful at evening to bring in a bough of the poplar or the red willow, when she would exclaim, "Oh, this is very acceptable; this is a change, for one gets tired eating white fish always (meaning the poplar); but the carp (meaning the red willow) is a pleasant change".

On the whole, Iena was much pleased with his wife for her neatness and attention to the things in the lodge, and he lived a contented and happy man. Being industrious, she made him beautiful bags from the bark of trees, and dressed the skins of the animals he killed in the most skilful manner. When spring opened, they found themselves blessed with two children, one of them resembling the father and the other the mother. One day the father made a bow and arrows for the child that resembled him, who was a son, saying, "My son, you will use these arrows to shoot at the little beavers when they begin to swim about the rivers". The mother, as soon as she heard this, was highly displeased; and taking her children, unknown to her husband, left the lodge in the night. A small river ran near the lodge, which the woman approached with her children. She built a dam across the stream, erected a lodge of earth, and lived after the manner of the beavers.

When the hunter awoke, he found himself alone in his lodge, and his wife and children absent. He immediately made diligent search after them, and at last discovered their retreat on the river. He approached the place of their habitation, and throwing himself prostrate on the top of the lodge, exclaimed, "Shingisshenaun tshee neeboyaun". (Here I will lie until I die.) The woman allowed the children to go close to their father, but not to touch him; for, as soon as they came very near, she would draw them away again, and in this manner she continued to torment him a long time. The husband laid in this situation until he was almost starved, when a young female approached him, and thus accosted him: "Look here; why are you keeping yourself in misery, and thus starving yourself? Eat this", reaching him a little mokuk containing fresh raspberries which she had just gathered. As soon as the beaveress, his former wife, beheld this, she began to abuse the young woman, and said to her, "Why do you wish to show any kindness to that *animal* that has but two legs? You will soon repent it." She also made sport of the young woman, saying, "Look at her; she has a long nose, and she is just like a bear". The young woman, who was all the time a bear in disguise, hearing herself thus reproached, broke down the dam of the beaver, let the water run out, and nearly killed the beaver herself. Then turning to the man, she thus addressed him: "Follow me; I will be kind to you. Follow me closely. You must be courageous, for there are three persons who are desirous of marrying me, and will oppose you. Be careful of yourself. Follow me nimbly, and, just as we approach the lodge, put your feet in the prints of mine, for I have eight sisters who will do their utmost to divert your attention and make you lose the way. Look neither to the right nor the left, but enter the lodge just as I do, and take your seat where I do." As they proceeded they came in sight of a

large lodge, when he did as he had been directed, stepping in her tracks. As they entered the lodge the eight sisters clamorously addressed him. "Oh, Ogidahkumigo (this term means a man that lives on the surface of the earth, as contradistinguished from beings living under ground) has lost his way", and each one invited him to take his seat with her, desiring to draw him from their sister. The old people also addressed him as he entered, and said, "Oh, make room for our son-in-law". The man, however, took his seat by the side of his protectress, and was not farther importuned.

As they sat in the lodge, a great rushing of waters, as of a swollen river, came through the centre of it, which also brought in its course a large stone, and left it before the man. When the water subsided, a large white bear came in, and taking up the stone, bit it, and scratched it with his paws, saying, "This is the manner in which I would handle Ogidahkumigo if I was jealous." A yellow bear also entered the lodge and did the same. A black bear followed and did the same. At length the man took up his bow and arrows, and prepared to shoot at the stone, saying, "This is the way I would treat Odanamekumigo (He who lives in the city under ground), if I was jealous." He then drew up his bow and drove his arrow into the stone. Seeing this, the bears turned around, and with their eyes fixed on him, stepped backward and left the lodge, which highly delighted the woman. She exulted to think that her husband had conquered them.

Finally, one of the old folks made a cry, and said, "Come, come! there must be a gathering of provisions for the winter." So they all took their *cossoes,* or bark dishes, and departed to gather acorns for the winter. As they departed, the old man said to his daughter, "Tell Ogidahkumigo to go to the place where your sisters have gone, and let him select one of them, so that, through her aid, he may have some food for himself during the winter; but be sure to caution him to be very careful, when he is taking the skin from the animal, that he does not cut the flesh." No sooner had the man heard this message, than he selected one of his sisters-in-law; and when he was taking the skin from her, for she was all the while an enchanted female bear, although careful, he cut her a little upon one of her arms, when she jumped up, assumed her natural form, and ran home. The man also went home, and found her with her arm bound up, and quite unwell.

At second cry was then made by the master of the lodge: "Come, come! seek for winter quarters;" and they all got ready to separate for the season. By

67

this time the man had two children, one resembling himself and the other his wife. When the cry was made, the little boy who resembled his father was in such a hurry in putting on his mocassins, that he misplaced them, putting the mocassin of the right foot upon the left. And this is the reason why the foot of the bear is turned in.

They proceeded to seek their winter quarters, the wife going before to point the way. She always selected the *thickest* part of the forest, where the child resembling the father found it difficult to get along; and he never failed to cry out and complain. Iena then went in the advance, and sought the open plain, whereupon the child resembling the mother would cry out and complain, because she disliked an *open* path. As they were encamping, the woman said to her husband, "Go and break branches for the lodge for the night." He did so; but when she looked at the *manner* in which her husband broke the branches, she was very much offended, for he broke them *upward* instead of *downward*. "It is not only very awkward," said she, "but we will be found out; for the Ogidahkumigoes (People who live above ground) will see where we have passed by the branches we have broken." To avoid this, they agreed to change their route, and were finally well established in their winter quarters. The wife had sufficient food for her child, and would now and then give the dry berries she had gathered in the summer to her husband.

One day, as spring drew on, she said to her husband, "I must boil you some meat," meaning her own paws, which bears suck in the month of April. She had all along told him, during the winter, that she meant to resume her real shape of a female bear, and to give herself up to the Ogidahkumigoes, to be killed by them, and that the time of their coming was near at hand. It came to pass, soon afterward, that a hunter discovered her retreat. She told her husband to move aside, "for," she added, "I am now giving myself up." The hunter fired and killed her.

Iena then came out from his hiding-place, and went home with the hunter. As they went, he instructed him what he must hereafter do when he killed bears. "You must," said he, "never cut the flesh in taking off the skin, nor hang up the feet with the flesh when drying it. But you must take the head and feet, and decorate them handsomely, and place tobacco on the head, for these animals are very fond of this article, and on the *fourth day* they come to life again."

68

Sheem
or the forsaken boy

A solitary lodge stood on the banks of a remote lake. It was near the hour of sunset. Silence reigned within and without. Not a sound was heard but the low breathing of the dying inmate and head of this poor family. His wife and three children surrounded his bed. Two of the latter were almost grown up; the other was a mere child. All their simple skill in medicine had been exhausted to no effect. They moved about the lodge in whispers, and were waiting the departure of the spirit. As one of the last acts of kindness, the skin door of the lodge had ·been thrown back to admit the fresh air. The poor man felt a momentary return of strength, and, raising himself a little, addressed his family.

"I leave you in a world of care, in which it has required all my strength and skill to supply you food, and protect you from the storms and cold of a severe climate. For you, my partner in life, I have less sorrow in parting, because I am persuaded you will not remain long behind me, and will therefore find the period of your sufferings shortened. But you, my children! my poor and forsaken children, who have just commenced the career of life, who will protect you from its evils? Listen to my words! Unkindness, ingratitude, and every wickedness is in the scene before you. It is for this cause that, years ago, I withdrew from my kindred and my tribe, to spend my days in this lonely spot. I have contented myself with the company of your mother and yourselves during seasons of very frequent scarcity and want, while your kindred, feasting in a scene where food is plenty, have caused the forests to echo with the shouts of successful war. I gave up these things for the enjoyment of peace. I wished to shield you from the bad examples you would inevitably have followed. I have seen you, thus far, grow up in innocence. If we have sometimes suffered bodily want, we have escaped pain of mind. We have been kept from scenes of rioting and bloodshed.

"My career is now at its close. I will shut my eyes in peace, if you, my children, will promise me to cherish each other. Let not your mother suffer during the few days that are left to her; and I charge you, on no account, to forsake your youngest brother. Of him I give you both my dying charge to take a tender care." He sank exhausted on his pallet. The family waited a moment, as if expecting to hear something farther; but, when they came to his side, the spirit had taken its flight.

The mother and daughter gave vent to their feelings in lamentations. The elder son witnessed the scene in silence. He soon exerted himself to supply, with the bow and net, his father's place. Time, however, wore away heavily. Five moons had filled and waned, and the sixth was near its full, when the mother also died. In her last moments she pressed the fulfilment of their promise to their father, which the children readily renewed, because they were yet free from selfish motives.

The winter passed; and the spring, with its enlivening effects in a northern hemisphere, cheered the drooping spirits of the bereft little family. The girl, being the eldest, dictated to her brothers, and seemed to feel a tender and sisterly affection for the youngest, who was rather sickly and delicate. The other boy soon showed symptoms of restlessness and ambition, and addressed the sister as follows: "My sister, are we always to live as if there were no other human beings in the world? Must I deprive myself of the pleasure of associating with my own kind? I have determined this question for myself. I shall seek the villages of men, and you cannot prevent me."

The sister replied: "I do not say no, my brother, to what you desire. We are not prohibited the society of our fellow-mortals; but we are told to cherish each other, and to do nothing independent of each other. Neither pleasure nor pain ought, therefore, to separate us, especially from our younger brother, who, being but a child, and weakly withal, is entitled to a double share of our affection. If we follow our separate gratifications, it will surely make us neglect him, whom we are bound by vows, both to our father and mother, to support." The young man received this address in silence. He appeared daily to grow more restiff and moody, and one day, taking his bow and arrows, left the lodge and never returned.

Affection nerved the sister's arm. She was not so ignorant of the forest arts as to let her brother want. For a long time she administered to his necessities, and supplied a mother's cares. At length, however, she began to be weary of solitude and of her charge. No one came to be a witness of her assiduity, or to let fall a single word in her native language. Years, which added to her strength and capability of directing the affairs of the household, brought with them the irrepressible desire of society, and made solitude irksome. At this point, selfishness gained the ascendency of her heart; for, in meditating a change in her mode of life, she lost sight of her younger brother, and left him to be provided for by contingencies.

One day, after collecting all the provisions she had been able to save for emergencies, after bringing a quantity of wood to the door, she said, to her little brother: "My brother, you must not stray from the lodge. I am going to seek our elder brother. I shall be back soon." Then, taking her bundle, she set off in search of habitations. She soon found them, and was so much taken up with the pleasures and amusements of social life, that the thought of her brother was almost entirely obliterated. She accepted proposals of marriage; and, after that, thought still less of her hapless and abandoned relative.

Meantime her elder brother had also married, and lived on the shores of the same lake whose ample circuit contained the abandoned lodge of his father and his forsaken brother. The latter was soon brought to the pinching turn of his fate. As soon as he had eaten all the food left by his sister, he was obliged to pick berries and dig up roots. These were finally covered by the snow. Winter came on with all its rigours. He was obliged to quit the lodge in search of other food. Sometimes he passed the night in the clefts of old trees or caverns, and ate the refuse meals of the wolves. The latter, at last, became his only resource; and he became so fearless of these animals that he would sit close by them while they devoured their prey. The wolves, on the other hand, became so familiar with his face and form, that they were undisturbed by his approach; and, appearing to sympathize with him in his outcast condition, would always leave something for his repast. In this way he lived till spring. As soon as the lake was free from ice, he followed his new-found friends to the shore. It happened, the same day, that his elder brother was fishing in his canoe, a considerable distance out in the lake, when he thought he heard the cries of a child on the shore, and wondered how any could exist on so bleak and barren a part of the coast. He listened again attentively, and distinctly heard the cry repeated. He made for shore as quick as possible, and, as he approached land, discovered and recognised his little brother, and heard him singing.

At the termination of his song, which was drawn out with a peculiar cadence, he howled like a wolf. The elder brother was still more astonished, when, getting nearer shore, he perceived his poor brother partly transformed into that animal. He immediately leaped on shore, and strove to catch him in his arms, soothingly saying, "My brother, my brother, come to me". But the boy eluded his grasp, crying as he fled, "Neesia, neesia", and howling in the intervals.

The elder brother, conscience stricken, and feeling his brotherly affection strongly return, with redoubled force exclaimed, in great anguish, "My brother! my brother! my brother!"

But, the nearer he approached, the more rapidly the transformation went on; the boy alternately singing and howling, and calling out the name, first of his brother, and then of his sister, till the change was completely accomplished, when he exclaimed, "I am a wolf!" and bounded out of sight.

Iadilla
or the
origin of the robin

An old man had an only son named *Iadilla,* who had come to that age which is thought to be most proper to make the long and final fast, that is to secure through life a guardian genius or spirit. In the influence of this choice, it is well known, our people have relied for their prosperity in after life; it was, therefore, an event of deep importance.

The old man was ambitious that his son should surpass all others in whatever was deemed most wise and great among his tribe; and, to fulfil his wishes, he thought it necessary that he should fast a much longer time than any of those persons, renowned for their prowess or wisdom, whose fame he coveted. He therefore directed his son to prepare, with great ceremony, for the important event. After he had been in the sweating lodge and bath several times, he ordered him to lie down upon a clean mat, in a little lodge expressly prepared for him; telling him, at the same time, to endure his fast like a man, and that, at the expiration of *twelve* days, he should receive food and the blessing of his father.

The lad carefully observed this injunction, lying with perfect composure, with his face covered, awaiting those mystic visitations which were to seal his good or evil fortune. His father visited him regularly every morning, to encourage him to perseverance, expatiating at length on the honour and renown that would attend him through life if he accomplished the full term prescribed. To these admonitions and encouragements the boy never replied, but lay, without the least sign of discontent or murmuring, until the ninth day, when he addressed his father as follows:

"My father, my dreams forebode evil. May I break my fast now, and at a more propitious time make a new fast?"

The father answered:

"My son, you know not what you ask. If you get up now, all your glory will depart. Wait patiently a little longer. You have but three days yet to accomplish your desire. You know it is for your own good, and I encourage you to persevere."

The son assented; and, covering himself closer, he lay till the eleventh day, when he repeated his request. Very nearly the same answer was given him by his father, who added that the next day he would himself prepare his first meal, and bring it to him. The boy remained silent, but lay as motionless as a corpse. No one would have known he was living but by the gentle heaving of his breast.

The next morning, the father, elated at having gained his end, prepared a repast for his son, and hastened to set it before him. On coming to the door, he was surprised to hear his son talking to himself. He stooped to listen; and, looking through a small aperture, was more astonished when he beheld, his son painted with vermilion over all his breast, and in the act of finishing his work by laying on the paint as far back on his shoulders as he could reach with his hands, saying, at the same time, to himself, "My father has destroyed my fortune as a man. He would not listen to my requests. He will be the loser. I shall be for ever happy in my new state, for I have been obedient to my parent; he alone will be the sufferer, for my guardian spirit is a just one; though not propitious to me in the manner I desired, he has shown me pity in another way; he has given me another shape; and now I must go."

At this moment the old man broke in, exclaiming, "My son! my son! I pray you leave me not." But the young man, with the quickness of a bird, had flown to the top of the lodge, and perched himself on the highest pole, having been changed into a beautiful robin redbreast.

He looked down upon his father with pity beaming in his eyes, and addressed him as follows: "Regret not, my father, the change you behold. I shall be happier in my present state than I could have been as a man. I shall always be the friend of men, and keep near their dwellings. I shall ever be happy and contented; and although I could not gratify your wishes as a warrior, it will be my daily aim to make you amends for it as a harbinger of peace and joy. I will cheer you by my songs, and strive to inspire in others the joy and lightsomeness I feel in my present state. This will be some compensation to you for the loss of the glory you expected. I am now free from the cares and pains of human life. My food is spontaneously furnished by the mountains and fields, and my pathway of life is in the bright air." Then stretching himself on his toes, as if delighted with the gift of wings, he carolled one of his sweetest songs, and flew away into a neighbouring grove.

The enchanted mocassins

There once lived a little boy with his sister, entirely alone, in an uninhabited country. He was called the Boy that carries the Ball on his Back, from an idea of his having supernatural powers. This boy was constantly in the habit of meditating, and asking within himself whether there were other and similar beings to themselves on the earth. When he grew up to manhood, he asked his sister if she knew of any human beings besides themselves. She replied that she did; and that there was, at a great distance, a large village. As soon as he heard this, he said to his sister, "I am now a young man, and very much in want of a partner;" and he asked his sister to make him several pairs of moccasins. She complied with his request; and, as soon as he received the moccasins, he took up his war-club and set out in quest of the distant village. He travelled on, till at length he came to a small wigwam, and, on looking into it, discovered a very old woman seeting alone by the fire. As soon as she saw the stranger, she invited him in, and thus addressed him: "My poor grandchild, I suppose you are one of those who seek for the distant village, from which no person has ever yet returned. Unless your guardian is more powerful than the guardian of your predecessors, you too will share a similar fate to theirs. Be careful to provide yourself with the Ozhebahguhnun—the bones they use in the medicine dance, without which you cannot succeed." After she had thus spoken, she gave him the following directions for his journey. "When you come near to the village which you seek, you will see in the centre a large lodge, in which the chief of the village, who has two daughters, resides. Before the door you will see a great tree, which is smooth and destitute of bark. On this tree, about the height of a man from the ground, a small lodge is suspended, in which these two daughters dwell. It is here so many have been destroyed. Be wise, my grandchild, and abide strictly by my directions." The old woman then gave him the Ozhebahguhnun, which would cause his success. Placing them in his bosom, he continued his journey, till at length he arrived at the sought-for village; and, as he was gazing around him, he saw both the tree and the lodge which the old woman had mentioned. Immediately he bent his steps for the tree, and approaching, he endeavoured to reach the suspended lodge. But all his efforts were vain; for as often as he attempted to reach it, the tree began to tremble, and soon shot up so that the lodge could hardly be perceived. Foiled as he was in all his attempts, he thought of his guardian, and changed himself into a small squirrel, that he might more easily accomplish his design. He then mounted the tree in quest of the lodge. After climbing for some time, he became fatigued and panted for breath; but, remembering the instructions which the old woman had given him, he took from his bosom one of the bones, and thrust it into the trunk of the tree on which he sat. In this way he quickly found relief; and, as often as he became fatigued, he repeated this; but whenever he came near the lodge and attempted to touch it, the tree would shoot up as before, and place the lodge beyond his reach. At length, the bones being exhausted, he began to despair, for the earth had long since vanished from his sight. Summoning all resolution, he determined to make another effort to reach the object of his wishes. On he went; yet, as soon as he came near the lodge and attempted to touch it, the tree again shook, but it had reached the arch of heaven, and could go no higher; so now he entered the lodge, and beheld the two sisters sitting opposite each other. He asked their names. The one on his left hand called herself Azhabee, (one who sits behind) and the one on the right Negahnahbee (one who sits before). Whenever he addressed the one on his left hand, the tree would tremble as before, and settle down to its former position. But when he addressed the one on his right hand, it would again shoot upward as before. When he thus discovered that, by addressing the one on his left hand, the tree would descend, he continued to do so until it had resumed its former position; then seizing his war-club, he thus addressed the sisters: "You, who have caused the death of so many of my brothers, I will now put an end to, and thus have revenge for the numbers you have destroyed." As he said this he raised the club and laid them dead at his feet. He then descended, and learning that these sisters had a brother living with their father, who would pursue him for the deed he had done, he set off at random, not knowing whither he went. Soon after, the father and mother of the young women visited their residence and found their remains. They immediately told their son Mudjikewis that his sisters had been slain. He replied, "The person who has done this must be the Boy that carries the Ball on his Back. I will pursue him, and have revenge for the blood of my sisters." "It is well, my son", replied the father. "The spirit of your life grant you success. I counsel you to be wary in the pursuit. It is a strong spirit who has done this injury to us, and he will try to deceive you in every way. Above all, avoid tasting food till you succeed; for if you break your fast before you see his blood, your power will be destroyed." So saying, they parted.

His son instantly set out in search of the murderer, who, finding he was closely pursued by the brother of the slain, climbed up into one of the tallest trees and shot forth his magic arrows. Finding that his pursuer was not turned back by his arrows, he renewed his flight; and when he found himself hard pressed, and his enemy close behind him, he transformed himself into the skeleton of a moose that had been killed, whose flesh had come off from his bones. He then remembered the moccasins which his sister had given him, which were enchanted. Taking a pair of them, he placed them near the skeleton. "Go", said he to them, "to the end of the earth".

The moccasins then left him and their tracks remained. Mudjikewis at length came to the skeleton of the moose, when he perceived that the track he had long been pursuing did not end there, so he continued to follow it up, till he came to the end of the earth, where he found only a pair of moccasins. Mortified that he had been outwitted by following a pair of moccasins instead of the object of his revenge, he bitterly complained, resolving not to give up the pursuit, and to be more wary and wise in scrutinizing signs. He then called to mind the skeleton he met with on his way, and concluded that *it* must be the object of his search. He retraced his steps towards the skeleton, but found, to his surprise, that it had disappeared, and that the tracks of *Onwee Bahmondung*, or he who carries the Ball, were in another direction. He now became faint with hunger, and resolved to give up the pursuit; but when he remembered the blood of his sisters, he determined again to pursue.

The other, finding he was closely pursued, now changed himself into a very old man, with two daughters, who lived in a large lodge in the centre of a beautiful garden, which was filled with everything that could delight the eye or was pleasant to the taste. He made himself appear so very old as to be unable to leave his lodge, and had his daughters to bring him food and wait on him. The garden also had the appearance of ancient occupancy, and was highly cultivated.

His pursuer continued on till he was nearly starved and ready to sink. He exclaimed, "Oh! I will forget the blood of my sisters, for I am starving." But again he thought of the blood of his sisters, and again he resolved to pursue, and be satisfied with nothing but the attainment of his right to revenge.

He went on till he came to the beautiful garden. He approached the lodge. As soon as the daughters of the owner perceived him, they ran and told their father that a stranger approached the lodge. Their father replied, "Invite him in, my children, invite him in." They quickly did so; and, by the command of their father, they boiled some corn and prepared other savoury food. Mudjike-wis had no suspicion of the deception. He was faint and weary with travel, and felt that he could endure fasting no longer. Without hesitancy, he partook heartily of the meal, and in so doing was overcome. All at once he seemed to forget the blood of his sisters, and even the village of his nativity. He ate so heartily as to produce drowsiness, and soon fell into a profound sleep. Onwee Bahmondung watched his opportunity, and, as soon as he found his slumbers sound, resumed his youthful form. He then drew the magic ball from his back, which turned out to be a heavy war-club, with one blow of which he put an end to his pursuer, and thus vindicated his title as the Wearer of the Ball.

The broken wing

There were six young falcons living in a nest, all but one whom, were still unable to fly, when it so happened that both the parent birds were shot by the hunters in one day. The young brood waited with impatience for their return; but night came, and they were left without parents and without food. Meeji-geeg-wona, or the Gray Eagle, the eldest, and the only one whose feathers had become stout enough to enable him to leave the nest, assumed the duty of stilling their cries and providing them with food, in which he was very successful. But, after a short time had passed, he, by an unlucky mischance, got one of his wings broken in pouncing upon a swan. This was the more unlucky, because the season had arrived when they were soon to go off to a southern climate to pass the winter, and they were only waiting to become a little stouter and more expert for the journey. Finding that he did not return, they resolved to go in search of him, and found him sorely wounded and unable to fly.

"Brothers," he said, "an accident has befallen me, but let not this prevent your going to a warmer climate. Winter is rapidly approaching, and you cannot remain here. It is better that I alone should die than for you all to suffer miserably on my account." "No! no!" they replied, with one voice, "we will not forsake you; we will share your sufferings; we will abandon our journey, and take care of you, as you did of us, before we were able to take care of ourselves. If the climate kills you, it shall kill us. Do you think we can so soon forget your brotherly care, which has surpassed a father's, and even a mother's kindness? Whether you live or die, we will live or die with you."

They sought out a hollow tree to winter in, and contrived to carry their wounded nestmate there; and, before the rigours of winter set in, they had stored up food enough to carry them through its severities. To make it last the better, two of the number went off south, leaving the other three to watch over, feed, and protect the wounded bird. Meeji-geeg-wona in due time recovered from his wound, and he repaid their kindness by giving them such advice and instruction in the art of hunting as his experience had qualified him to impart. As spring advanced, they began to venture out of their hiding-place, and were all successful in getting food to eke out their winter's stock, except the youngest, who was called Peepi-geewi-zains, or the Pigeon Hawk. Being small and foolish, flying hither and yon, he always came back without anything. At last the Gray Eagle spoke to him, and demanded the cause of his ill luck. "It is not my smallness or weakness of body," said he, "that prevents my bringing home flesh as well as my brothers. I kill ducks and other birds every time I go out; but, just as I get to the woods, a large Ko-ko-ko-ho (Owl) robs me of my prey." "Well! don't despair, brother," said Meeji-geeg-wona. "I now feel my strength perfectly recovered, and I will go out with you to-morrow," for he was the most courageous and warlike of them all.

Next day they went forth in company, the elder seating himself near the lake. Peepi-geewi-zains started out, and soon pounced upon a duck.

"Well done!" thought his brother, who saw his success; but, just as he was getting to land with his prize, up came a large white owl from a tree, where he had been watching, and laid claim to it. He was about wresting it from him, when Meeji-geeg-wona came up, and, fixing his talons in both sides of the owl, flew home with him.

The little pigeon hawk followed him closely, and was rejoiced and happy to think he had brought home something at last. He then flew in the owl's face, and wanted to tear out his eyes, and vented his passion in abundance of reproachful terms.   "Softly," said the Gray Eagle; "do not be in such a passion, or exhibit so revengeful a disposition; for this will be a lesson to him not to tyrannize over any one who is weaker than himself for the future." So, after giving him good advice, and telling him what kind of herbs would cure his wounds, they let the owl go.

While this act was taking place, and before the liberated owl had yet got out of view, two visiters appeared at the hollow tree. They were the two nestmates, who had just returned from the south after passing the winter there, and they were thus all happily reunited, and each one soon chose a mate and flew off to the woods. Spring had now revisited the north. The cold winds had ceased, the ice had melted, the streams were open, and the forest began rapidly to put on its vernal hue. "But it is in vain," said the old man who related this story, "it is in vain that spring returns, if we are not thankful to the Master of Life who has preserved us through the winter. Nor does that man answer the end for which he was made who does not show a kind and charitable feeling to all who are in want or sickness, especially to his blood relations. These six birds only represent one of our empoverished northern families of children, who had been deprived of both their parents and the aid of their elder brother nearly at the same time."

The three cranberries

Three cranberries were living in a lodge together. One was green, one white, and one red. They were sisters. There was snow on the ground; and as the men were absent, they felt afraid, and began to say to each other, "What shall we do if the wolf comes?" "I," said the green one, "will climb up a shingoub (spruce) tree." "I," said the white one, "will hide myself in the kettle of boiled hommony;" "and I," said the red one, "will conceal myself under the snow." Presently the wolves came, and each one did as she had said. But only one of the three had judged wisely. The wolves immediately ran to the kettle and ate up the corn, and, with it, the white cranberry. The red one was trampled to pieces by their feet, and her blood spotted the snow. But she who had climbed the thick spruce-tree escaped notice, and was saved.

Paradise opened
to the Indians

An Indian of the Lenapee (Delawares) tribe, anxious to know the Master of Life, resolved, without mentioning his design to any one, to undertake a journey to Paradise, which he knew to be God's residence. But, to succeed in his project, it was necessary for him to know the way to the celestial regions. Not knowing any person who, having been there himself, might aid him in finding the road, he commenced juggling, in the hope of drawing a good augury from his dream.

The Indian, in his dream, imagined that he had only to commence his journey, and that a continued walk would take him to the celestial abode. The next morning very early, he equipped himself as a hunter, taking a gun, powder-horn, ammunition, and a boiler to cook his provisions. The first part of his journey was pretty favourable; he walked a long time without being discouraged, having always a firm conviction that he should attain his aim. Eight days had already elapsed without his meeting with any one to oppose his desire. On the evening of the eighth day, at sunset, he stopped as usual on the bank of a brook, at the entrance of a little prairie, a place which he thought favourable for his night's encampment. As he was preparing his lodging, he perceived at the other end of the prairie three very wide and well-beaten paths; he thought this somewhat singular; he, however, continued to prepare his wigwam, that he might shelter himself from the weather. He also lighted a fire. While cooking, he found that, the darker it grew, the more distinct were those paths. This surprised, nay, even frightened him; he hesitated a few moments. Was it better for him to remain in his camp, or seek another at some distance? While in this incertitude, he remembered his juggling, or rather his dream. He thought that his only aim in undertaking his journey was to see the Master of Life. This restored him to his senses. He thought it probable that one of those three roads led to the place which he wished to visit. He therefore resolved upon remaining in his camp until the morrow, when he would, at random, take one of them. His curiosity, however, scarcely allowed him time to take his meal; he left his encampment and fire, and took the widest of the paths. He followed it until the middle of the day without seeing anything to impede his progress; but, as he was resting a little to take breath, he suddenly perceived a large fire coming from under ground. It excited his curiosity; he went towards it to see what it might be; but, as the fire appeared to increase as he drew nearer, he was so overcome with fear, that he turned back and took the widest of the other two paths. Having followed it for the same space of time as he had the first, he perceived a similar spectacle. His fright, which had been lulled by the change of road, awoke, and he was obliged to take the third path, in which he walked a whole day without seeing anything. All at once, a mountain of a marvellous whiteness burst upon his sight. This filled him with astonishment; nevertheless, he took courage and advanced to examine it. Having arrived at the foot, he saw no signs of a road. He became very sad, not knowing how to continue his journey. In this conjuncture, he looked on all sides and perceived a female seated upon the mountain; her beauty was dazzling, and the whiteness of her garments surpassed that of snow. The woman said to him in his own language, "You appear surprised to find no longer a path to reach your wishes. I know that you have for a long time longed to see and speak to the Master of Life; and that you have undertaken this journey purposely to see him. The way which leads to his abode is upon this mountain. To ascend it, you must undress yourself completely, and leave all your accoutrements and clothing at the foot. No person shall injure them. You will then go and wash yourself in the river which I am now showing you, and

afterward ascend the moutain."

The Indian obeyed punctually the woman's words; but one difficulty remained. How could he arrive at the top of the mountain, which was steep, without a path, and as smooth as glass? He asked the woman how he was to accomplish it. She replied, that if he really wished to see the Master of Life, he must, in mounting, only use his left hand and foot. This appeared almost impossible to the Indian. Encouraged, however, by the female, he commenced ascending, and succeeded after much trouble. When at the top, he was astonished to see no person, the woman having disappeared. He found himself alone, and without a guide. Three unknown villages were in sight; they were constructed on a different plan from his own, much handsomer, and more regular. After a few moments' reflection, he took his way towards the handsomest. When about half way from the top of the moutain, he recollected that he was naked, and was afraid to proceed; but a voice told him to advance, and have no apprehensions; that, as he had washed himself, he might walk in confidence. He proceeded without hesitation to a place which appeared to be the gate of the village, and stopped until some one came to open it. While he was considering the exterior of the village, the gate opened, and the Indian saw coming towards him a handsome man dressed all in white, who took him by the hand, and said he was going to satisfy his wishes by leading him to the presence of the Master of Life.

The Indian suffered himself to be conducted, and they arrived at a place of unequalled beauty. The Indian was lost in admiration. He there saw the Master of Life, who took him by the hand, and gave him for a seat a hat bordered with gold. The Indian, afraid of spoiling the hat, hesitated to sit down; but, being again ordered to do so, he obeyed without reply.

The Indian being seated, God said to him, "I am the Master of Life, whom thou wishest to see, and to whom thou wishest to speak. Listen to that which I will tell thee for thyself and for all the Indians. I am the Maker of Heaven and earth, the trees, lakes, rivers, men, and all that thou seest or hast seen on the earth or in the heavens; and because I love you, you must do my will; you must also avoid that which I hate; I hate you to drink as you do, until you lose your reason; I wish you not to fight one another; you take two wives, or run after other people's wives; you do wrong; I hate such conduct; you should have but one wife, and keep her until death. When you go to war, you juggle, you sing the medicine song, thinking you speak to me; you deceive yourselves;

it is to the Manito that you speak; he is a wicked spirit who induces you to evil, and, for want of knowing me, you listen to him.

"The land on which you are, I have made for you, not for others: wherefore do you suffer the whites to dwell upon your lands? Can you not do without them? I know that those whom you call the children of your great Father supply your wants. But, were you not wicked as you are, you would not need them. You might live as you did before you knew them. Before those whom you call your brothers had arrived, did not your bow and arrow maintain you? You needed neither gun, powder, nor any other object. The flesh of animals was your food, their skins your raiment. But when I saw you inclined to evil, I removed the animals into the depths of the forests, that you might depend on your brothers for your necessaries, for your clothing. Again become good and do my will, and I will send animals for your sustenance. I do not, however, forbid suffering among you your Father's children; I love them, they know me, they pray to me; I supply their own wants, and give them that which they bring to you. Not so with those who are come to trouble your possessions. Drive them away; wage war against them. I love them not. They know me not. They are my enemies, they are your brothers' enemies. Send them back to the lands I have made for them. Let them remain there.

"Here is a written prayer which I give thee; learn it by heart, and teach it to all the Indians and children." (The Indian, observing here that he could not read, the Master of Life told him that, on his return upon earth, he should give it to the chief of his village, who would read it, and also teach it to him, as also to all the Indians.) "It must be repeated", said the Master of Life, "morning and evening. Do all that I have told thee, and announce it to all the Indians as coming from the Master of Life. Let them drink but one draught, or two at most, in one day. Let them have but one wife, and discontinue running after other people's wives and daughters. Let them not fight one another. Let them not sing the medicine song, for in singing the medicine song they speak to the evil spirit. Drive from your lands," added the Master of Life, "those dogs in red clothing; they are only an injury to you. When you want anything, apply to me, as your brothers do, and I will give to both. Do not sell to your brothers that which I have placed on the earth as food. In short, become good, and you shall want nothing. When you meet one another, bow, and give one another the hand of the heart. Above all, I command thee to repeat, morning and evening, the prayer which I have given thee."

The Indian promised to do the will of the Master of Life, and also to recommend it strongly to the Indians; adding that the Master of Life should be satisfied with them.

His conductor then came, and, leading him to the foot of the mountain, told him to take his garments and return to his village; which was immediately done by the Indian.

His return much surprised the inhabitants of the village, who did not know what had become of him. They asked him whence he came; but, as he had been enjoined to speak to no one until he saw the chief of the village, he motioned to them with his hand that he came from above. Having entered the village, he went immediately to the chief's wigwam, and delivered to him the prayer and laws intrusted to his care by the Master of Life.

Peeta Kway
or the tempest

There once lived a woman called Monedo Kway (female spirit or prophetess) on the sand mountains called "the Sleeping Bear" of Lake Michigan, who had a daughter as beautiful as she was modest and discreet. Everybody spoke of the beauty of this daughter. She was so handsome that her mother feared she would be carried off, and to prevent it she put her in a box on the lake, which was tied by a long string to a stake on the shore. Every morning the mother pulled the box ashore, and combed her daughter's long, shining hair, gave her food, and then put her out again on the lake.

One day a handsome young man chanced to come to the spot as the moment she was receiving her morning's attentions from her mother. He was struck with her beauty, and immediately went home and told his feelings to his uncle, who was a great chief and a powerful magician. "My nephew," replied the old man, "go to the mother's lodge, and sit down in a modest manner, whithout saying a word. You need not ask her the question. But whatever *you think* she will understand, and what *she thinks* in answer you will also understand." The young man did so. He sat down, with his head dropped in a thoughtful manner, without uttering a word. He then thought, "I wish she would give me her daughter." Very soon he understood the mother's thoughts in reply. "Give you my daughter?" thought she; "*you!* No, indeed, my daughter shall never marry *you*." The young man went away and reported the result to his uncle. "Woman without good sense,", said he, "who is she keeping her daughter for? Does she think she will marry the Mudjikewis? (A term indicative of the heir or successor to the first place in power.)

"Proud heart! we will try her magic skill, and see whether she can withstand our power." The pride and haughtiness of the mother was talked of by the spirits living on that part of the lake. They met together and determined to exert their power in humbling her. For this purpose they resolved to raise a great storm on the lake. The water began to toss and roar, and the tempest became so severe, that the string broke, and the box floated off through the straits down Lake Huron, and struck against the sandy shores at its outlet. The place where it struck was near the lodge of a superannuated old spirit called Ishkwon Daimeka, or the keeper of the gate of the lakes. He opened the box and let out the beautiful daughter, took her into his lodge, and married her.

When the mother found that her daughter had been blown off by the storm, she raised very loud cries and lamented exceedingly. This she continued to do for a long time, and would not be comforted. At length, after two or three years, the spirits had pity on her, and determined to raise another storm and bring her back. It was even a greater storm than the first; and when it began to wash away the ground and encroach on the lodge of Ishkwon Daimeka, she leaped into the box, and the waves carried her back to the very spot of her mother's lodge on the shore. Monedo Equa was overjoyed; but when she opened the box, she found that her daughter's beauty had almost all departed. However, she loved her still because she was her daughter, and now thought of the young man who had made her the offer of marriage. She sent a formal message to him, but he had altered his mind, for he knew that she had been the wife of another. "*I* marry your daughter?" said he; "*your* daughter! No, indeed! I shall never marry her."

The storm that brought her back was so strong and powerful, that it tore away a large part of the shore of the lake, and swept off Ishkwon Daimeka's lodge, the fragments of which, lodging in the straits, formed those beautiful islands which are scattered in the St. Clair and Detroit rivers. The old man

94

himself was drowned, and his bones are buried under them. They heard him singing as he was driven off on a portion of his lodge; some fragments of his words are still repeated, which show what his thoughts were in the midst of his overthrow.

Bokwewa
or the humpback

Bokwewa and his brother lived in a secluded part of the country. They were considered as Manitoes, who had assumed mortal shapes. Bokwewa was the most gifted in supernatural endowments, although he was deformed in person. His brother partook more of the nature of the present race of beings. They lived retired from the world, and undisturbed by its cares, and passed their time in contentment and happiness.

Bokwewa (I. e., the sudden stopping of a voice), owing to his deformity, was very domestic in his habits, and gave his attention to household affairs. He instructed his brother in the manner of pursuing game, and made him acquainted with all the accomplishments of a sagacious and expert hunter. His brother possessed a fine form, and an active and robust constitution; and felt a disposition to show himself off among men. He was restiff in his seclusion, and showed a fondness for visiting remote places.

One day he told his brother that he was going to leave him; that he wished to visit the habitations of men, and procure a wife. Bokwewa objected to his going; but his brother overruled all that he said, and he finally departed on his travels. He travelled a long time. At length he fell in with the footsteps of men. They were moving by encampments, for he saw several places where they had encamped. It was in the winter. He came to a place where one of their number had died. They had placed the corpse on a scaffold. He went to it and took it down. He saw that it was the corpse of a beautiful young woman. "She shall be my wife!" he exclaimed.

He took her up, and placing her on his back, returned to his brother: "Brother," he said, "cannot you restore her to life? Oh, do me that favour!" Bokwewa said he would try. He performed numerous ceremonies, and at last succeeded in restoring her to life. They lived very happily for some time. Bokwewa was extremely kind to his brother, and did everything to render his life happy. Being deformed and crippled, he always remained at home, while his brother went out to hunt. And it was by following his directions, which were those of a skilful hunter, that he always succeeded in returning with a good store of meat.

One day he had gone out as usual, and Bokwewa was sitting in his lodge, on the opposite side of his brother's wife, when a tall, fine young man entered, and immediately took the woman by the hand and drew her to the door. She resisted and called on Bokwewa, who jumped up to her assistance. But their joint resistance was unavailing; the man succeeded in carrying her away. In the scuffle, Bokwewa had his hump back much bruised on the stones near the door. He crawled into the lodge and wept very sorely, for he knew that it was a powerful Manito who had taken the woman.

When his brother returned he related all to him exactly as it had happened. He would not taste food for several days. Sometimes he would fall to weeping for a long time, and appeared almost beside himself. At last he said he would go in search of her. Bokwewa tried to dissuade him from it, but he insisted.

"Well!" said he, "since you are bent on going, listen to my advice. You will have to go south. It is a long distance to the residence of your captive wife, and there are so many charms and temptations in the way, I am afraid you will be led astray by them, and forget your errand. For the people whom you will see in that country do nothing but amuse themselves. They are very idle, gay, and effeminate, and I am fearful they will lead you astray. Your journey is besets with difficulties. I will mention one or two things, which you must be on your guard against. In the course of your journey, you will come to a large grapevine lying across your way. You must not even taste its fruits, for it is poisonous. Step over it. It is a snake. You will next come to something that looks like bear's fat, transparent and tremulous. Don't taste it, or you will be overcome by the pleasures of those people. It is frog's eggs. These are snares laid by the way for you."

He said he would follow the advice, and bid farewell to his brother. After travelling a long time, he came to the enchanted grapevine. It looked so tempting, he forgot his brother's advice and tasted the fruit. He went on till he came to the frog's eggs. The substance so much resembled bear's fat that he tasted it. He still went on. At length he came to a very extensive plain. As he emerged from the forest the sun was setting, and cast its scarlet and golden shades over all the plain. The air was perfectly calm, and the whole prospect had the air of an enchanted land. The most inviting fruits and flowers spread out before the eye. At a distance he beheld a large village, filled with people without number, and as he drew near he saw women beating corn in silver mortars. When they saw him approaching, they cried out, "Bokwewa's brother has come to see us." Throngs of men and women, gayly dressed, came out to meet him. He was soon overcome by their flatteries and pleasures, and he was not long afterward seen beating corn with their women (the strongest proof of effeminacy), although his wife, for whom he had mourned so much, was in that Indian metropolis.

Meantime Bokwewa waited patiently for the return of his brother. At length, after the lapse of several years, he sat out in search of him, and arrived in safety among the luxuriant people of the South. He met with the same allurements on the road, and the same flattering reception that his brother did. But he was above all temptations. The pleasures he saw had no other effect upon him than to make him regret the weakness of mind of those who were led away by them. He shed tears of pity to see that his brother had laid aside the arms of a hunter, and was seen beating corn with the women.

He ascertained where his brother's wife remained. After deliberating some time, he went to the river where she usually came to draw water. He there changed himself into one of those hair-snakes which are sometimes seen in running water. When she came down, he spoke to her, saying "Take me up; I am Bokwewa." She then scooped him out and went home. In a short time the Manito who had taken her away asked her for water to drink. The lodge in which they lived was partitioned. He occupied a secret place, and was never seen by any one but the woman. She handed him the water containing the hair-snake, which he drank, with the snake, and soon after was a dead Manito.

Bokwewa then resumed his former shape. He went to his brother, and used every means to reclaim him. But he would not listen. He was so much taken up with the pleasures and dissipations into which he had fallen, that he refused to give them up, although Bokwewa, with tears, tried to convince him of his foolishness, and to show him that those pleasures could not endure for a long time. Finding that he was past reclaiming, Bokwewa left him, and disappeared for ever.

Aggo Dah Gauda
or the man
with his leg tied up

Aggo Dah Gauda had one leg looped up to his thigh, so that he was obliged to get along by hopping. He had a beautiful daughter, and his chief care was to secure her from being carried off by the king of the buffaloes. It was a peculiarity in which he differed from other Indians, that he lived in a log house, and he advised his daughter to keep in doors and never got out into the neighbourhood for fear of being stolen away.

One sunshiny morning Aggo Dah Gauda prepared to go out a fishing, but before he left the lodge reminded his daughter of her strange and persecuting lover. "My daughter", said he, "I am going out to fish, and as the day will be a pleasant one, you must recollect that we have an enemy near, who is constantly going about, and do not expose yourself out of the lodge." When he had reached his fishing ground, he heard a voice singing at a distance the following strains, in derision of him.

He saw no one, but suspecting it to come from his enemies the buffaloes, he hastened his return.

Let us now see what happened to the daughter. Her father had not been

long absent from the lodge, when she thought in her mind, [ke in ain dum] it is hard to be thus for ever kept in doors. The spring is now coming on, and the days are so sunny and warm, that it would be very pleasant to sit out doors. But my father says it would be dangerous. I know what I will do. I will get on the top of the house, and there I can comb and dress my hair. She accordingly got up on the roof of the small house, and busied herself in untying and combing her beautiful hair. For her hair was not only of a fine glossy quality, but was so long that it reached down on the ground, and hung over the eaves of the house, as she sat dressing it. She was so intent upon this, that she forgot all ideas of danger, till it was too late to escape. For, all of a sudden, the king of the buffaloes came dashing on, with his herd of followers, and taking her between his horns, away he cantered over the plains, plunged into a river that bounded his land, and carried her safely to his lodge, on the other side. Here he paid every attention to gain her affections, but all to no purpose, for she sat pensively and disconsolate in the lodge among the other females, and scarcely ever spoke, and took no part in the domestic cares of her lover the king. He, on the contrary did every thing he could think of to please her and win her affections. He told the others in his lodge to give her every thing she wanted, and to be careful not to displease her. They set before her the choicest food. They gave her the seat of honour in the lodge. The king himself went out hunting to obtain the most dainty bits of meat, both of animals and wild fowl. And not content with these proofs of his attachment he fasted himself, and would often take his pib be gwun (Indian flute), and sit near the lodge indulging his mind in repeating a few pensive notes.

In the mean time Aggo Dah Gauda came home, and finding his daughter had been stolen, determined to get her back. For this purpose he immediately set out. He could easily track the king, until he came to the banks of the river, and saw that he had plunged in and swam over. But there had been a frosty night or two since, and the water was so covered with thin ice, so that he could not walk on it. He determined to encamp till it became solid, and then crossed over and pursued the trail. As he went along he saw branches broken off and strewed behind, for these had been purposely cast along by the daughter, that the way might be found. And the manner in which she had accomplished it, was this. Her hair was all untied when she was caught up, and being very long, it caught on the branches as they darted along, and it was these twigs that she broke off for signs to her father. When be came to the king's lodge it

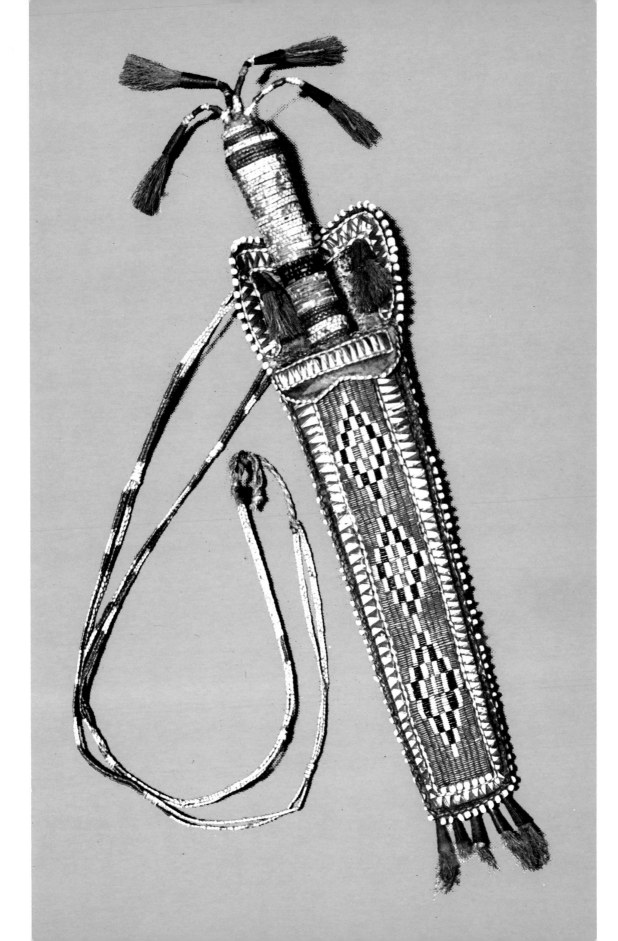

was evening. Carefully approaching it, he peeped through the sides and saw his daughter sitting disconsolately. She immediately caught his eye, and knowing that it was her father come for her, she all at once appeared to relent in her heart, and asking for the dipper, said to the king, "I will go and get you a drink of water". This token of submission delighted him, and he waited with impatience for her return. At last he went out with his followers, but nothing could be seen or heard of the captive daughter. They sallied out in the plains, but had not gone far, by the light of the moon, when a party of hunters, headed by the father-in-law of Aggo Dah Gauda, set up their yells in their rear, and a shower of arrows was poured in upon them. Many of their numbers fell, but the king being stronger and wifter than the rest, fled toward the west, and never again appeared in that part of the country.

While all this was passing Aggo Dah Gauda, who had met his daughter the moment she came out of the lodge, and being helped by his guardian spirit, took her on his shoulders and hopped off, a hundred steps in one, till he reached the stream, crossed it, and brought back his daughter in triumph to his lodge.

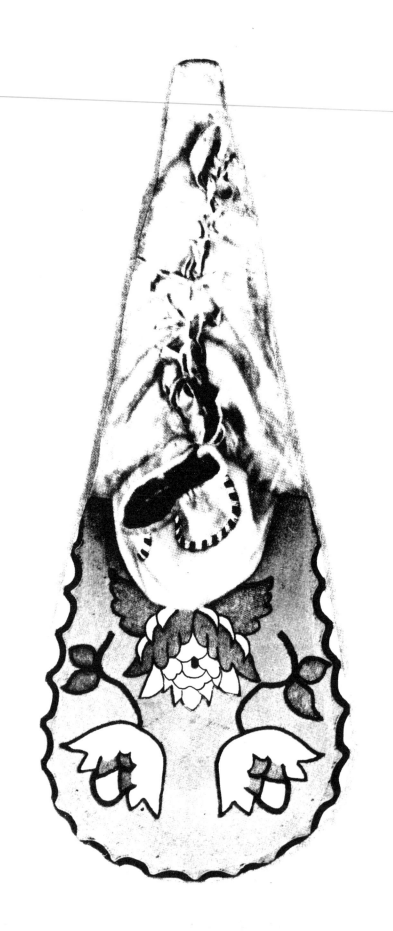

The two ghosts
or a trial of feeling

There lived a hunter in the north who had a wife and one child. His lodge stood far off in the forest, several days journey from any other. He spent his days in hunting, and his evenings in relating to his wife the incidents that had befallen him. As game was very abundant he found no difficulty in killing as much as they wanted. Just in all his acts, he lived a peaceful and happy life.

One evening during the winter season, it chanced that he remained out later than usual, and his wife began to feel uneasy, for fear some accident had befallen him. It was already dark. She listened attentively and at last heard the sound of approaching footsteps. Not doubting it was her husband, she went to the door and beheld two strange females. She bade them enter, and invited them to remain.

She observed that they were total strangers in the country. There was something so peculiar in their looks, air, and manner, that she was uneasy in their company. They would not come near the fire; they sat in a remote part of the lodge, were shy and taciturn, and drew their garments about them in such a manner as nearly to hide their faces. So far as she could judge, they were pale, hollow-eyed, and long-visaged, very thin and emaciated. There was but little light in the lodge, as the fire was low, and served by its fitful flashes, rather to increase than dispel their fears. "Merciful spirit!" cried a voice from the opposite part of the lodge, "there are two corpses clothed with garments". The hunter's wife turned arround, but seeing nobody, she concluded the sounds were but gust of wind. She trembled, and was ready to sink to the earth.

Her husband at this moment entered and dispelled her fears. He threw down the carcass of a large fat deer. "Behold what a fine and fat animal", cried the mysterious females, and they immediately ran and pulled off pieces of the whitest fat (the fat of animals is esteemed by the N.A. Indians among the choicest parts), which they ate with greediness. The hunter and his wife looked on with astonishment, but remained silent. They supposed their guests might have been famished. Next day, however, the same unusual conduct was repeated. The strange females tore off the fat and devoured it with eagerness. The third day the hunter thought he would anticipate their wants by tying up a portion of the fattest pieces for them, which he placed on the top of his load. They accepted it, but still appeared dissatisfied, and went to the wife's portion and tore off more. The man and his wife felt surprised at such rude and unaccountable conduct, but they remained silent, for they respected their guests, and had observed that they had been attended with marked good luck during the residence of these mysterious visiters.

In other respects the deportment of the females was strictly unexceptionable. They were modest, distant, and silent. They never uttered a word during the day. At night they would occupy themselves in procuring wood, which they carried to the lodge, and then returning the implements exactly to the places in which they had found them, resume their places without speaking. They were never known to stay out until daylight. They never laughed or jested.

The winter had nearly passed away, without anything uncommon happening, when one evening the hunter stayed out very late. The moment he entered and laid down his day's hunt as usual before his wife, the two females began to tear off the fat, in so unceremonious a way, that her anger was excited. She constrained herself, however, in a measure, but did not conceal her feelings, although she said but little. The guests observed the excited state of her mind, and became unusually reserved and uneasy. The good hunter saw the change, and carefully inquired into the cause, but his wife denied having used any hard words. They retired to their couches, and he tried to compose himself to sleep, but could not, for the sobs and sighs of the two females were incessant. He arose on his couch and addressed them as follows:

"Tell me," said he, "what is it that gives you pain of mind, and causes you to utter those sighs. Has my wife given you offence, or trespassed on the rights of hospitality?"

They replied in the negative. "We have been treated by you with kindness and affection. It is not for any slight we have received, that we weep. Our mission is not to you only. We come from the land of the dead to test mankind, and to try the sincerity of the living. Often we have heard the bereaved by death say that if the dead could be restored, they would devote their lives to make them happy. We have been moved by the bitter lamentations which have reached the place of the dead, and have come to make proof of the sincerity of those who have lost friends. Three moons were allotted us by the Master of life to make the trial. More than half the time had been successfully past, when the angry feelings of your wife indicated the irksomeness you felt at our presence, and has made us resolve on our departure."

They continued to talk to the hunter and his wife, gave them instructions as to a future life, and pronounced a blessing upon them.

"There is one point", they added, "of which we wish to speak. You have thought our conduct very strange in rudely possessing ourselves of the choicest parts of your hunt. *That* was the point of trial selected to put you to. It is the wife's peculiar privilege. For another to usurp it, we knew to be the severest trial of her, and consequently of your temper and feelings. We know your manners and customs, but we came to prove you, not by a compliance with them, but a violation of them. Pardon us. We are the agents of him who sent us. Peace to your dwelling, adieu!"

When they ceased total darkness filled the lodge. No object could be seen. The inmates heard the door open and shut, but they never saw more of the two ghosts.

The hunter found the success which they had promised. He became celebrated in the chase, and never wanted for any thing. He had many children, all of whom grew up to manhood, and health, peace, and long life were the rewards of his hospitality.

Pah-Hah-Undootah or the Red Head

As spring approaches, the Indians return from their wintering grounds to their villages, engage in feasting, soon exhaust their stock of provisions, and begin to suffer for the want of food. Such of the hunters as are of an active and enterprising cast of character, take the occasion to separate from the mass of the population, and remove to some neighbouring locality in the forest, which promises the means of subsistence during this season of general lassitude and enjoyment.

Among the families who thus separated themselves, on a certain occasion, there was a man called Odshedoph Waucheentongah, or the Child of Strong Desires, who had a wife and one son. After a day's travel he reached an ample wood with his family, which was thought to be a suitable place to encamp. The wife fixed the lodge, while the husband went out to hunt. Early in the evening he returned with a deer. Being tired and thirsty he asked his son to go to the river for some water. The son replied that it was dark and he was afraid. He urged him to go, saying that his mother, as well as himself, was tired, and the distance to the water was very short. But not persuasion was of any avail.

He refused to go. "Ah, my son," said the father, at last, "if you are afraid to go to the river you will never kill the Red Head."

The boy was deeply mortified by this observation. It seemed to call up all his latent energies. He mused in silence. He refused to eat, and made no reply when spoken to.

The next day he asked his mother to dress the skin of the deer, and make it into moccasins for him, while he busied himself in preparing a bow and arrows. As soon as these things were done, he left the lodge one morning at sunrise, without saying a word to his father or mother. He fired one of his arrows into the air, which fell westward. He took that course, and at night coming to the spot where the arrow had fallen, was rejoiced to find it piercing the heart of a deer. He refreshed himself with a meal of the venison, and the next morning fired another arrow. After travelling all day, he found it also in another deer. In this manner he fired four arrows, and every evening found that he had killed a deer. What was very singular, however, was, that he left the arrows sticking in the carcases, and passed on without withdrawing them. In consequence of this, he had no arrow for the fifth day, and was in great distress at night for the want of food. At last he threw himself upon the ground in despair, concluding that he might as well perish there as go farther. But he had not lain long before he heard a hollow, rumbling noise, in the ground beneath him. He sprang up, and discovered at a distance the figure of a human being, walking with a stick. He looked attentively and saw that the figure was walking in a wide beaten path, in a prairie, leading from a lodge to a lake. To his surprise this lodge was at no great distance. He approached a little nearer and concealed himself. He soon discovered that the figure was no other than that of the terrible witch, Wok-On-Kahtohn-Zooeyah' Pee-Kah-Haitchee, or the little old woman who makes war. Her path to the lake was perfectly smooth and solid, and the noise our adventurer had heard, was caused by the striking of her walking staff upon the ground. The top of this staff was decorated with a string of the toes and bills of birds of every kind, who at every stroke of the stick, fluttered and sung their various notes in concert.

She entered her lodge and laid off her mantle, which was entirely composed of the scalps of women. Before folding it, she shook it several times, and at every shake the scalps uttered loud shouts of laughter, in which the old hag joined. Nothing could have frightened him more than this horrific exhibition. After laying by the cloak she came directly to him. She informed him that she had known him from the time he left his father's lodge, and watched his movements. She told him not to fear or despair, for she would be his friend and protector. She invited him into her lodge, and gave him a supper. During the repast, she inquired of him his motives for visiting her. He related his history, stated the manner in which he had been disgraced, and the difficulties he laboured under. She cheered him with the assurance of her friendship, and told him he would be a brave man yet.

She then commenced the exercise of her power upon him. His hair being very short she took a large leaden comb, and after drawing it through his hair several times, it became of a handsome feminine length. She then proceeded to dress him as a female, furnishing him with the necessary garments, and decorated his face with paints of the most beautiful dye. She gave him a bowl of shining metal. She directed him to put in his girdle a blade of scented sword-grass, and to proceed the next morning to the banks of the lake, which was no other than that over which the Red Head reigned. Now Pah-Hau-Undootah, or the Red Head, was a most powerful sorcerer and the terror of all the country, living upon an island in the centre of the lake.

She informed him that there would be many Indians on the island, who as soon as they saw him use the shining bowl to drink with, would come and solicit him to be their wife, and to take him over to the island. These offers he was to refuse, and say that he had come a great distance to be the wife of the Red Head, and that if the chief could not come for her in his own canoe, she should return to her village. She said that as soon as the Red Head heard of this, he would come for her in his own canoe, in which she must embark. On reaching the island he must consent to be his wife, and in the evening induce him to take a walk out of the village, when he was to take the first opportunity to cut off his head with the blade of grass. She also gave him general advice how he was to conduct himself to sustain his assumed character of a woman. His fear would scarcely permit him to accede to this plan, but the recollection of his father's words and looks decided him.

Early in the morning, he left the witch's lodge, and took the hard beaten path to the banks of the lake. He reached the water at a point directly opposite the Red Head's village. It was a beautiful day. The heavens were clear, and the sun shone out in the greatest effulgence. He had not been long there, having sauntered along the beach, when he displayed the glittering bowl, by dipping water from the lake. Very soon a number of canoes came off from the

island. The men admired his dress, and were charmed with his beauty, and a great number made proposals of marriage. These he promptly declined, agreeably to the concerted plan. When the facts were reported to the Red Head, he ordered his canoe to be put in the water by his chosen men, and crossed over to see this wonderful girl. As he came near the shore, he saw that the ribs of the sorcerer's canoe were formed of living rattlesnakes, whose heads pointed outward to guard him from enemies. Our adventurer had no sooner stepped into the canoe than they began to hiss and rattle, which put him in a great fright. But the magician spoke to them, after which they became pacified and quiet, and all at once they were at the landing upon the island. The marriage immediately took place, and the bride made presents of various valuables which had been furnished by the old witch.

As they were sitting in the lodge surrounded by friends and relatives, the mother of the Red Head regarded the face of her new daughter-in-law for a long time with fixed attention. From this scrutiny she was convinced that this singular and hasty marriage augured no good to her son. She drew her husband aside and disclosed to him her suspicions: This can be no female, said she, the figure and manners, the countenance, and more especially the expression of the eyes, are, beyond a doubt, those of a man. Her husband immediately rejected her suspicions, and rebuked her severely for the indignity offered to her daughter-in-law. He became so angry, that seizing the first thing that came to hand, which happened to be his pipe stem, he beat her unmercifully. This act requiring to be explained to the spectators, the mock bride immediately rose up, and assuming an air of offended dignity, told the Red Head that after receiving so gross an insult from his relatives he could not think of remaining with him as his wife, but should forthwith return to his village and friends. He left the lodge followed by the Red Head, and walked until he came upon the beach of the island, near the spot where they had first landed. Red Head entreated him to remain. He pressed him by every motive which he thought might have weight, but they were all rejected. During this conference they had seated themselves upon the ground, and Red Head, in great affliction, reclined his head upon his fancied wife's lap. This was the opportunity ardently sought for, and it was improved to the best advantage. Every means was taken to lull him to sleep, and partly by a soothing manner, and partly by a seeming compliance with his request, the object was at last attained. Red Head fell into a sound sleep. Our aspirant, for the glory of a brave man, then drew his blade of grass, and drawing it once across the neck of the Red Head completely severed the head from the body.

He immediately stripped off his dress, seized the bleeding head, and plunging into the lake, swam safely over to the main shore. He had scarcely reached it, when looking back he saw amid the darkness, the torches of persons come out in search of the new-married couple. He listened till they had found the headless body, and he heard their piercing shrieks of sorrow, as he took his way to the lodge of his kind adviser.

She received him with rejoicing. She admired his prudence, and told him his bravery could never be questioned again. Lifting up the head, she said he need only have brought the scalp. She cut off a small piece for herself, and told him he might now return with the head, which would be evidence of an achievement that would cause the Indians to respect him. In your way home, she said, you will meet with but one difficulty. Maunkah Keesh Woccaung, or the Spirit of the Earth, requires an offering from those who perform extraordinary achievements. As you walk along in a prairie, there will be an earthquake. The earth will open and divide the prairie in the middle. Take this partridge and throw it into the opening, and instantly spring over it. All this happened precisely as it had been foretold. He cast the partridge into the crevice and leapt over it. He then proceeded without obstruction to a place near his village, where he secreted his trophy. On entering the village he found his parents had returned from the place of their spring encampment, and were in great sorrow for their son, whom they supposed to be lost. One and another of the young men had presented themselves to the disconsolate parents, and said, "Look up, I am your son." Having been often deceived in this manner, when their own son actually presented himself, they sat with their heads down, and with their eyes nearly blinded with weeping. It was some time before they could be prevailed upon to bestow a glance upon him. It was still longer before they recognised him for their son; when he recounted his adventures they believed him mad. The young men laughed at him. He left the lodge and soon returned with his trophy. It was soon recognised. All doubts of the reality of his adventures now vanished. He was greeted with joy and placed among the first warriors of the nation. He finally became a chief, and his family were ever after respected and esteemed.

Leelinau
or the lost daughter

Leelinau was the favourite daughter of an able hunter who lived near the base of the lofty highlands called Kaug Wudjoo, on the shore of Lake Superior. From her earliest youth she was observed to be pensive and timid, and to spend much of her time in solitude and fasting. Whenever she could leave her father's lodge she would fly to remote haunts and recesses in the woods, or sit upon some high promontory of rock overlooking the lake. In such places she was supposed to invoke her guardian spirit. But amid all the sylvan haunts, so numerous in a highly picturesque section of country, none had so great attractions for her mind as a forest of pines, on the open shore, called Manitowak, or the Sacred Grove. It was one of those consecrated places which are supposed to be the residence of the Puk Wudj Ininee, or little wild men of the woods, and Mishen Imokinakog, or turtle-spirits, two classes of minor spirits or fairies who love romantic scenes. Owing to this notion, it was seldom visited by Indians, who attribute to these imaginary beings a mischievous agency. And whenever they were compelled by stress of weather to make a landing on this part of the coast, they never failed to leave an offering of tobacco, or some other article.

To this fearful spot Leelinau had made her way at an early age, gathering strange flowers or plants, which she would bring home to her parents, and relate to them all the little incidents that had occurred in her rambles. Although they discountenanced her visits to the place, they were unable to restrain them, for they did not wish to lay any violent commands upon her. Her attachment to the spot, therefore, increased with her age. If she wished to propitiate her spirits to procure pleasant dreams, or any other favour, she repaired to the Manitowok. If her father remained out later than usual, and it was feared he had been overwhelmed by the tempest, or met with some other accident, she offered up her prayers at the Manitowok. It was there that she fasted, supplicated, and strolled. And she spent so much of her time there, that her parents began to suspect some bad spirit had enticed her to its haunts, and thrown a charm around her which she was unable to resist. This conjecture was confirmed by her mother (who had secretly followed her) overhearing her repeat sentiments like these.

The effect of these visits was to render the daughter dissatisfied with the realities of life, and to disqualify her for an active and useful participation in its duties. She became melancholy and taciturn. She had permitted her mind to dwell so much on imaginary scenes, that she at last mistook them for realities, and sighed for an existence inconsistent with the accidents of mortality. The consequence was, a disrelish for all the ordinary sources of amusement and employment, which engaged her equals in years. When the girls of the neighbouring lodges assembled to play at the favourite game of pappus-e-kowaun (a game played with sticks and two small blocks on a string by females), before the lodge door, Leelinau would sit vacantly by, or enter so feebly into the spirit of the play, as to show plainly that it was irksome to her. Again, in the evening, when the youths and girls formed a social ring around the lodge, and the pie-peendjigun (a game played with a piece of perforated leather and a bone), passed rapidly from hand to hand, she either handed it along without attempting to play, or if she played, it was with no effort to swell her count. Her parents saw that she was a prey to some secret power, and attempted to divert her in every way they could. They favoured the attentions paid to her by a man much her senior in years, but who had the reputation of great activity, and was the eldest son of a neighbouring chief. But she could not be persuaded to listen to the proposal. Supposing her aversion merely the result of natural timidity, her objections were not deemed of a serious character; and in a state of society

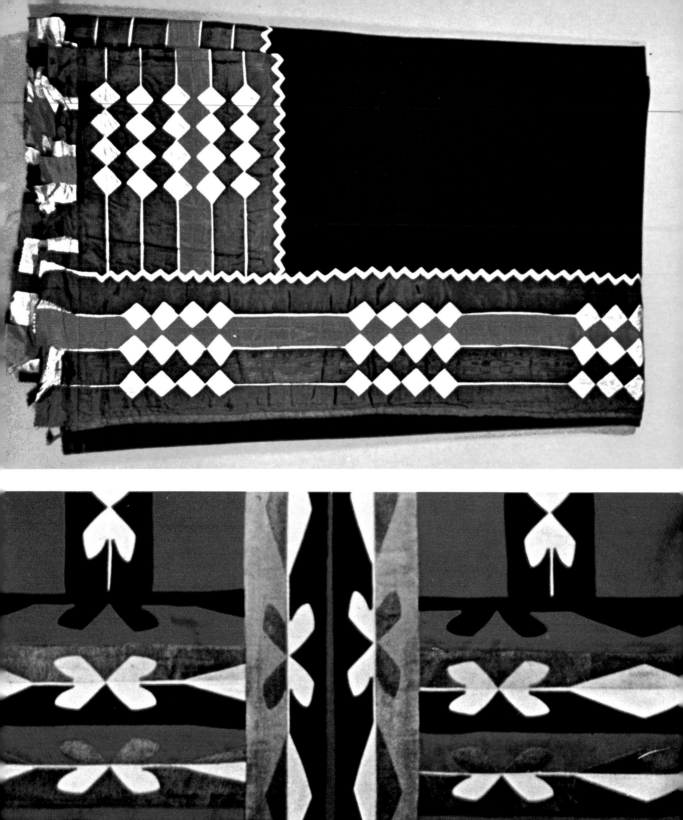

where matches are left very much in the hands of the parents, they proceeded to make the customary arrangements for the union. The young man was informed, through his parents, that his offer had been favourably received. The day was fixed for the marriage visit to the lodge, and the persons who were to be present were invited. As the favourable expression of the will of the parents had been explicit given, and compliance was as certainly expected, she saw no means of frustrating the object, but by a firm declaration of her sentiments. She told her parents that she could never consent to the match, and that her mind was unalterably made up.

It has been her custom to pass many of her hours in her favourite place of retirement, under a low, broad-topped young pine, whose leaves whispered in the wind. Thither she now went, and while leaning pensively against its trunk, she fancied she heard articulate sounds. Very soon they became more distinct, and appeared to address her.

Her fancy confirmed all she heard as the words of sober truth. She needed nothing more to settle her purpose.

On the evening preceding the day fixed for her marriage, she dressed herself in her best garments. She arranged her hair according to the fashion of her tribe, and put on the ornaments she possessed. Thus robed, she assumed an air of unwonted gayety, as she presented herself before her parents. I am going, said she, to meet my little lover, the chieftain of the green plume, who is waiting for me at the Spirit Grove; and her countenance expressed a buoyant delight, which she had seldom evinced. They were quite pleased with these evidences of restored cheerfulness, supposing she was going to act some harmless freak. "I am going", said she, to her mother, as she left the lodge, "from one who has watched my infancy, and guarded my youth. Who has given me medicine when I was sick, and prepared me food when I was well. I am going from a father who has ranged the forest to procure the choicest skins for my dress, and kept his lodge supplied with the best food of the chase. I am going from a lodge which has been my shelter from the storms of winter, and my shield from the heats of summer. Adieu! adieu!" she cried as she skipped lightly over the plain.

So saying she hastened to the confines of the fairy haunted grove. As it was her common resort, no alarm was entertained, and the parents confidently waited her return with the sunset hour. But as she did not arrive, they began to feel uneasy. Darkness approached, and no daughter returned. They now

lighted torches of pine wood, and proceeded to the gloomy forest of pines, but were wholly unsuccessful in the search. They called aloud upon her name, but the echo was their only reply. Next day the search was renewed, but with no better success. Suns rose and set, but they rose and set upon a bereaved father and mother, who were never afterward permitted to behold a daughter whose manners and habits they had not sufficiently guarded, and whose inclinations they had, in the end, too violently thwarted.

One night a party of fishermen, who were spearing fish near the Spirit Grove, descried something resembling a female figure standing on the shore. As the evening was mild, and the waters calm, they cautiously paddled their canoe ashore, but the slight ripple of the water excited alarm. The figure fled, but they recognised, in the shape and dress, as she ascended the bank, the lost daughter, and they saw the green plumes of her lover waving over his forehead, as he glided lightly through the forest of young pines.

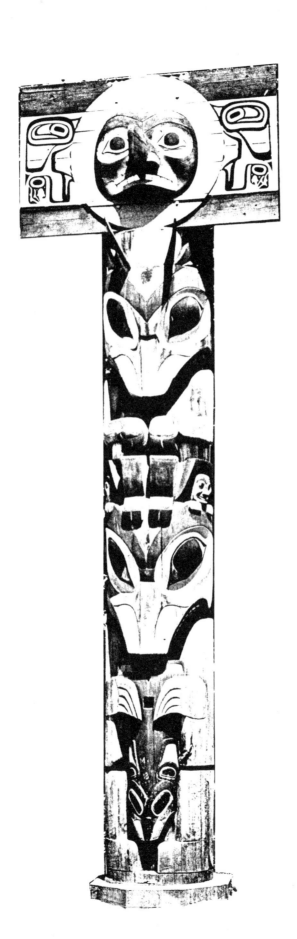

Puck Wudj Ininee

There was a time when all the inhabitants of the earth had died, excepting two helpless children, a baby boy, and a little girl. When their parents died, these children were asleep. The little girl, who was the elder, was the first to awake. She looked around her, but seeing nobody besides her little brother, who lay asleep, she quietly resumed her bed. At the end of ten days her brother moved without opening his eyes. At the end of ten days more he changed his position, lying on the other side.

The girl soon grew up to woman's estate, but the boy increased in stature very slowly. It was a long time before he could even creep. When he was able to walk, his sister made him a little bow and arrows, and suspended around his neck a small shell, saying, you shall be called Wa-Dais-Ais-Imid, or He of the Little Shell. Every day he would go out with his little bow shooting at the small birds. The first bird he killed was a tomtit. His sister was highly pleased when he took it to her. She carefully skinned and stuffed it, and put it away for him. The next day he killed a red squirrel. His sister preserved this too. The third day he killed a partridge (Peéna), which she stuffed and set up. After this, he acquired more courage, and would venture some distance from home. His skill and success as a hunter daily increased, and he killed the deer, bear, moose, and other large animals inhabiting the forest. In fine he became a great hunter.

He had now arrived to maturity of years, but remained a perfect infant in stature. One day walking about he came to a small lake. It was in the winter season. He saw a man on the ice killing beavers. He appeared to be a giant. Comparing himself to this great man he appeared no bigger than an insect. He seated himself on the shore, and watched his movements. When the large man had killed many beavers, he put them on a hand sled, which he had, and pursued his way home. When he saw him retire, he followed him, and wielding his magic shell, cut off the tail of one of the beavers, and ran home with his trophy. When the tall stranger reached his lodge, with his sled load of beavers, he was surprised to find the tail of one of them gone, for he had not observed the movements of the little hero of the shell.

The next day Wa-Dais-Ais-Imid, went to the same lake. The man had already fixed his load of beavers on his *odaw'bon* or sled, and commenced his return. But he nimbly ran forward, and overtaking him, succeeded, by the same means, in securing another of the beaver's tails. When the man saw that he had lost another of this most esteemed part of the animal, he was very angry. I wonder, said he, what dog it is, that has thus cheated me. Could I meet him, I would make his flesh quiver at the point of my lance. Next day he pursued his hunting at the beaver dam near the lake, and was followed again by the little man of the shell. On this occasion the hunter had used so much expedition, that he had accomplished his object, and nearly reached his home, before our tiny hero could overtake him. He nimbly drew his shell and cut off another beaver's tail. In all these pranks, he availed himself of his power of invisibility, and thus escaped observation. When the man saw that the trick had been so often repeated, his anger was greater than ever. He gave vent to his fellings in words. He looked carefully around to see whether he could discover any tracks. But he could find none. His unknown visiter had stepped so lightly as to leave no track.

Next day he resolved to disappoint him by going to his beaver pond very early. When Wa-Dais-Ais-Imid reached the place, he found the fresh traces of his work, but he had already returned. He followed his tracks, but failed to overtake him. When he came in sight of the lodge the stranger was in front of it, employed in skinning his beavers. As he stood looking at him, he thought, I will let him see me. Presently the man, who proved to be no less a personage than Manabozho, looked up and saw him. After regarding him with attention, "who are you, little man", said Manabozho. "I have a mind to kill you." The little hero of the shell replied, "If you were to try to kill me you could not do it."

When he returned home he told his sister that they must separate. "I must go away", said he, "it is my fate. You too", he added, "must go away soon. Tell me where you would wish to dwell." She said, "I would like to go to the breaking of daylight. I have always loved the east. The earliest glimpses of light are from that quarter, and it is, to my mind, the most beautiful part of the heavens. After I get there, my brother, whenever you see the clouds in that direction of various colours, you may think that your sister is painting her face."

"And I", said he, "my sister, shall live on the mountains and rocks. There I can see you at the earliest hour, and there the streams of water are clear, and the air pure. And I shall ever be called Puck Wudj Ininee, or the little wild man of the mountains."

"But", he resumed, "before we part for ever, I must go and try to find some Manitoes." He left her and travelled over the surface of the globe, and then went far down into the earth. He had been treated well wherever he went. At last he found a giant Manito, who had a large kettle, which was for ever boiling. The giant regarded him with a stern look, and then took him up in his hand, and threw him unceremoniously into the kettle. But by the protection of his personal spirit, he was shielded from harm, and with much ado got out of it and escaped. He returned to his sister, and related his rovings and misadventures. He finished his story by addressing her thus: "My sister, there is a Manito, at each of the four corners of the earth. (The opinion that the earth is a square and level plain, and that the winds blow from its four corners, is a very ancient eastern opinion.) There is also one above them, far in the sky, and last," continued he, "there is another; and wicked one, who lives deep down in the earth. We must now seperate. When the winds blow from the four corners of the earth you must then go. They will carry you to the place you wish. I got to the rocks and mountains, where my kindred will ever delight to dwell." He then took his ball stick, and commenced running up a high mountain, whooping as he went. Presently the winds blew, and as he predicted, his sister was borne by them to the eastern sky, where she has ever since been, and her name is the Morning Star.

Mishosha,
or the magician
of the lakes

In a early age of the world, when there were fewer inhabitants than there now are, there lived an Indian, in a remote place, who had a wife and two children. They seldom saw any one out of the circle of their own lodge. Animals were abundant in so secluded a situation, and the man found no difficulty in supplying his family with food.

In this way they lived in peace and happiness, which might have continued if the hunter had not found cause to suspect his wife. She secretly cherished an attachment for a young man whom she accidentally met one day in the woods. She even planned the death of her husband for his sake, for she knew if she did not kill her husband, her husband, the moment he detected her crime, would kill her.

The husband, however, eluded her project by his readiness and decision. He narrowly watched her movements. One day he secretly followed her footsteps into the forest, and having concealed himself behind a tree, he soon beheld a tall young man approach and lead away his wife. His arrows were in his hands, but he did not use them. He thought he would kill her the moment she returned. Meantime, he went home and sat down to think. At last he came to the determination of quitting her for ever, thinking that her own conscience would punish her sufficiently, and relying on her maternal feelings to take care of the two children, who were boys, he immediately took up his arms and departed.

When the wife returned she was disappointed in not finding her husband, for she had now concerted her plan, and intended to have despatched him. She waited several days, thinking he might have been led away by the chase, but finding he did not return, she suspected the true cause. Leaving her two children in the lodge, she told them she was going a short distance and would return. She then fled to her paramour and came back no more.

The children thus abandoned, soon made way with the food left in the lodge, and were compelled to quit it in search of more. The eldest boy, who was of an intrepid temper, was strongly attached to his brother, frequently carrying him when he became weary, and gathering all the wild fruit he saw. They wandered deeper and deeper into the forest, losing all traces of their former habitation, until they were completely lost in its mazes.

The eldest boy had a knife, with which he made a bow and arrows, and was thus enable to kill a few birds for himself and brother. In this manner they continued to pass on, from one piece of forest to another, not knowing whither they were going. At length they saw an opening through the woods, and were shortly afterward delighted to find themselves on the borders of a large lake. Here the elder brother busied himself in picking the seed pods of the wild rose, which he preserved as food. In the meantime, the younger brother amused himself by shooting arrows in the sand, one of which happened to fall into the lake. Panigwun (the end wing feather), the elder brother, not willing to lose the arrow, waded in the water to reach it. Just as he was about to grasp the arrow, a canoe passed up to him with great rapidity. An old man, sitting in the centre, seized the affrighted youth and placed him in the canoe. In vain the boy addressed him—"My grandfather, (a term of respect for old people), pray take my little brother also. Alone, I cannot go with you; he will starve if I leave him." Mishosha (the old man) only laughed at him. Then uttering the charm, Chemaun Poll, and giving his canoe a slap, it glided through the water with inconceivable swiftness. In a few moments they reached the habitation of the magician, standing on an island in the centre of the lake. Here he lived with his two daughters, who managed the affairs of his household. Leading

132

the young man up to the lodge, he addressed his eldest daughter. "Here," said he, "my daughter, I have brought a young man to be your husband." Husband! thought the young woman; rather another victim of your bad arts, and your insatiate enmity to the human race. But she made no reply, seeming thereby to acquiesce in her father's will.

The young man thought he saw surprise depicted in the eyes of the daughter, during the scene of this introduction, and determined to watch events narrowly. In the evening he overheard the two daughters in conversation. "There," said the eldest daughter, "I told you he would not be satisfied with his last sacrifice. He has brought another victim, under the pretence of providing me a husband. Husband, indeed! the poor youth will be in some horrible predicament before another sun has set. When shall we be spared the scenes of vice and wickedness which are daily taking place before our eyes."

Panigwun took the first opportunity of acquainting the daughters how he had been carried off, and been compelled to leave his little brother on the shore. They told him to wait until their father was asleep, then to get up and take his canoe, and using the charm he had obtained, it would carry him quickly to his brother. That he could carry him food, prepare a lodge for him, and be back before daybreak. He did, in every respect, as he had been directed— the canoe obeyed the charm, and carried him safely over, and after providing for the subsistence of his brother, told him that in a short time he should come for him. Then returning to the enchanted island, he resumed his place in the lodge, before the magician awoke. Once, during the night, Mishosha awoke, and not seeing his destined son-in-law, asked his daughter what had become of him. She replied that he had merely stepped out, and would be back soon. This satisfied him. In the morning, finding the young man in the lodge, his suspicions were completely lulled. "I see, my daughter," said he, "you have told the truth." As soon as the sun arose, Mishosha thus addressed the young man. "Come, my son, I have a mind to gather gulls' eggs. I know an island where there are great quantities, and I wish your aid in getting them." The young man saw no reasonable excuse; and getting into the canoe, the magician gave it a slap, and uttering a command, they were in an instant at the island. They found the shores strown with gulls' eggs, and the island full of birds of this species. "Go, my son", say the old man, "and gather the eggs, while I remain in the canoe."

But Panigwun had no sooner got ashore, than Michosha pushed his canoe a little from the land, and exclaimed—"Listen, ye gulls! you have long expected an offering from me. I now give you a victim. Fly down and devour him." Then striking his canoe, he left the young man to his fate.

The birds immediately came in clouds around their victim, darkening the air with their numbers. But the youth seizing the first that came near him, and drawing his knife, cut off its head. He immediately skinned the bird, and hung the feathers as a trophy on his breast. "Thus," he exclaimed, "will I treat every one of you who approaches me. Forbear, therefore, and listen to my words. It is not for you to eat human flesh. You have been given by the Great Spirit as food for man. Neither is it in the power of that old magician to do you any good. Take me on your backs and carry me to his lodge, and you shall see that I am not ungrateful." The gulls obeyed; collecting in a cloud for him to rest upon, and quickly flew to the lodge, where they arrived before the magician. The daughters were surprised at his return, but Mishosha, on entering the lodge, conducted himself as if nothing extraordinary had taken place. The next day he again addressed the youth:—"Come, my son," said he, "I will take you to an island covered with the most beautiful stones and pebbles, looking like silver. I wish you to assist me in gathering some of them. They will make handsome ornaments, and possess great medicinal virtues." Entering the canoe, the magician made use of his charm, and they were carried in a few moments to a solitary bay in an island, where there was a smooth sandy beach. The young man went ashore as usual, and began to search. "A little farther, a little farther," cried the old man. "Upon that rock you will get some fine ones." Then pushing his canoe from land—"Come, thou great king of fishes," cried the old man; "you have long expected an offering from me. Come, and eat the stranger whom I have just put ashore on your island." So saying, he commanded his canoe to return, and it was soon out of sight.

Immediately, a monstrous fish thrust his long snout from the water, crawling partially on the beach, and opening wide his jaws to receive his victim. "When!" exclaimed the young man, drawing his knife and putting himself in a threatening attitude, "when did you ever taste human flesh? Have a care of yourself. You were given by the Great Spirit to man, and if you, or any of your tribe eat human flesh, you will fall sick and die. Listen not to the words of that wicked man, but carry me back to his island, in return for which I will present you a piece of red cloth." The fish complied, raising his back out of the water,

134

to allow the young man to get on. Then taking his way through the lake, he landed his charge safely on the island before the return of the magician. The daughters were still more surprised to see that he had escaped the arts of their father the second time. But the old man on his return maintained his taciturnity and self-composure. He could not, however, help saying to himself—"What manner of boy is this, who is ever escaping from my power. But his spirit shall not save him. I will entrap him tomorrow. Ha, ha, ha!"

Next day the magician addressed the young man as follows: "Come, my son," said he, "you must go with me to procure some young eagles. I wish to tame then. I have discovered an island where they are in great abundance." When they had reached the island, Mishosha led him inland until they came to the foot of a tall pine, upon which the nests were. "Now, my son," said he, "clumb up this tree and bring down the birds." The young man obeyed. When he had with great difficulty got near the nest, "Now," exclaimed the magician, addressing the tree, "stretch yourself up and be very tall." The tree rose up at the command. "Listen, ye eagles," continued the old man, "you have long expected a gift from me. I now present you this boy, who has had the presumption to molest your young. Stretch forth your claws and seize him." So saying he left the young man to his fate, and returned.

But the intrepid youth drawing his knife, and cutting off the head of the first eagle that menaced him, raised his voice and exclaimed, "Thus will I deal with all who come near me. What right have you, ye ravenous birds, who were made to feed on beasts, to eat human flesh? Is it because that cowardly old canoe-man has bid you do so? He is an old woman. He can neither do you good nor harm. See, I have already slain one of your number. Respect my bravery, and carry me back that I may show you how I shall treat you." The eagles, pleased with his spirit, assented, and clustering thick around him formed a seat with their backs, and flew toward the island. As they crossed the water they passed over the magician, lying half asleep in his canoe.

The return of the young man was hailed with joy by the daughters, who now plainly saw that he was under the guidance of a strong spirit. But the ire of the old man was excited, although he kept his temper under subjection. He taxed his wits for some new mode of ridding himself of the youth, who had so successfully baffled his skill. He next invited him to go a hunting.

Taking his canoe, they proceeded to an island and built a lodge to shelter themselves during the night. In the mean while the magician caused a deep

Lone Buffalo

miniconi

fall of snow, with a storm of wind and severe cold. According to custom, the young man pulled off his moccasins and leggings and hung them before the fire to dry. After he had gone to sleep the magician, watching his opportunity, got up, and taking one moccasin and one legging, threw them into the fire. He then went to sleep. In the morning, stretching himself as he arose and uttering an exclamation of surprise, "My son," said he, "what has become of your moccasin and legging? I believe this is the moon in which fire attracts, and I fear they have been drawn in." The young man suspected the true cause of his loss, and rightly attributed it to a desing of the magician to freeze him to death on the march. But the maintained the strictest silence, and drawing his conaus over his head thus communed with himself: "I have full faith in the Manito who has preserved me thus far, I do not fear that he will forsake me in this cruel and emergency. Great is his power, and I invoke it now that he may enable me to prevail over this wicked enemy of mankind."

He then drew on the remaining moccasin and legging, and taking a dead coal from the fireplace, invoked his spirit to give it efficacy, and blackened his foot and legs as far as the lost garment usually reached. He then got up and announced himself ready for the march. In vain Mishosha led him through snows and over morasses, hoping to see the lad sink at every moment. But in this he was disappointed, and for the first time they returned home together.

Taking courage from this success, the young man now determined to try his own power, having previously consulted with the daughters. They all agreed that the life the old man led was detestable, and that whoever would rid the world of him, would entitle himself to the thanks of the human race.

On the following day the young man thus addressed his hoary captor. "My grandfather, I have often gone with you on perilous excursions and never murmured. I must now request that you will accompany me. I wish to visit my little brother, and to bring him home with me." They accordingly went on a visit to the main land, and found the little lad in the spot where he had been left. After taking him into the canoe, the young man again addressed the magician: "My grandfather, will you go and cut me a few of those red willows on the bank, I wish to prepare some smoking mixture." "Certainly, my son," replied the old man, "what you wish is not very hard. Ha, ha, ha! do you think me too old to get up there?" No sooner was Mishosha ashore, than the young man, placing himself in the proper position struck the canoe with his hand, and pronouncing the charm, N'chimaun Poll, the canoe immediately flew through the water on its return to the island. It was evening when the two brothers arrived, and carried the canoe ashore. But the elder daughter informed the young man that unless he sat up and watched the canoe, and kept his hand upon it, such was the power of their father, it would slip off and return to him. In the meantime the canoe slipped off and sought its master, who soon returned in high glee. "Ha, ha, ha! my son," said he; "you thought to play me a trick. It was very clever. But you see I am too old for you."

A short time after, the youth again addressed the magician. "My grandfather, I wish to try my skill in hunting. It is said there is plenty of game on an island not far off, and I have to request that you will take me there in your canoe." They accordingly went to the island and spent the day in hunting. Night coming on they put up a temporary lodge. When the magician had sunk into a profound sleep, the young man got up, and taking one of Mishosha's leggings and moccasins from the place where they hung, threw them into the fire, thus retaliating the artifice before played upon himself. He had discovered that the foot and leg were the only vulnerable parts of the magician's body. Having committed these articles to the fire, he besought his Manito that he would raise a great storm of snow, wind, and hail, and then laid himself down beside the old man. Consternation was depicted on the countenance of the latter, when he awoke in the morning and found his moccasin and legging missing. "I believe, my grandfather," said the young man, "that this is the moon in which fire attracts, and I fear your foot and leg garments have been drawn in." He saw him faltering at every step, and almost benumbed with cold, but encouraged him to follow, saying, we shall soon get through and reach the shore; although he took pains, at the same time, to lead him in roundabout ways, so as to let the frost take complete effect. At length the old man reached the brink of the island where the woods are succeeded by a border of smooth sand. But he could go no farther; his legs became stiff and refused motion, and he found himself fixed to the spot. He felt his legs growing downward like roots, the feathers of his turned to leaves, and a few seconds he stood a tall and stiff sycamore, learning toward the water. Panigwun leaped into the canoe, and pronouncing the charm, was soon transported to the island, where he related his victory to the daughters. They applauded the deed, agreed to put on mortal shapes, become wives to the two young men, and for ever quit the enchanted island. And passing immediately over the main land, they lived lives of happiness and peace.

The Weendigoes

Once there lived in a lonely forest, a man and his wife, who had a son. The father went out every day, according to the custom of the Indians, to hunt for food, to support his family. One day while he was absent, his wife, on going out of the lodge, looked toward the lake that was near, and saw a very large man walking on the water, and coming fast toward the lodge. He had already advanced so near that flight was useless. She thought to herself, what shall I say to the monster that will please him. As he came near, she ran in, and taking the hand of her son, a boy of three or four years old, led him out. Speaking very loud, "See, my son", said she, "your grandfather", and then added in a conciliatory tone, "he will have pity on us". The giant advanced, and said sneeringly, "Yes, my son". And then addressing the woman said, "Have you anything to eat". Fortunately the lodge was filled with meat of various kinds. The woman thought to please him by handing him some cooked meat, but he pushed it away in a dissatisfied manner, and took up the raw carcass of a deer, which he *glutted* up, sucking the bones, and drinking the blood.

When the hunter came home, he was surprised to see the monster, for he looked very frightful. He had again brought home the whole carcass of a deer, which he had no sooner put down than the cannibal seized it, tore it to pieces, and devoured it, as if it had been a mere mouthful. The hunter looked at him with fear and astonishment, telling his wife that he was afraid for their lives, as this monster was one whom Indians call Weendigo. He did not even dare to speak to him, nor did the cannibal say a word, but as soon as he had finished his meal, he laid himself down and fell asleep.

Early next morning he told the hunter that he should also go out hunting, and they went together. Toward evening they returned, the man bringing a deer, but the Weendigo brought home the bodies of two Indians, whom he had killed. He very composedly sat down and commenced tearing the limbs apart, breaking the bones with his teeth, and despatching them as easily as if they had been soft pieces of flesh. He was not even satisfied with that, but again took up the deer which the hunter had brought, to finish his supper, while the hunter and his family had to live on their dried meat.

In this manner the hunter and the Weendigo lived for some time, and it is remarkable that the monster never made an attempt on their lives, although the ground outside the lodge was white with the human bones he had cast out. He was always still and gloomy, and seldom spake to them. One evening he told the hunter that the time had now arrived for him to take his leave, but before doing so he would give him a charm, that would always make him successful in killing moose. This charm consisted of two arrows, and after giving them to the hunter he thanked him and his wife for their kindness, and departed, saying that he had all the world to travel over.

The hunter and his wife felt happy when freed from his presence, for they had expected, at every moment, to have been devoured by him. He tried the virtues of his arrows, and never failed to be successful in their use. They had lived in this manner for a year, when a great evil befell them. The hunter was absent one day when his wife, on going out of the lodge, saw something like a black cloud approaching. She looked till it came near, when she perceived that it was another Weendigo. She apprehended no danger, thinking he would treat them as the first one had done. In this she was wholly mistaken. Unluckily they had but a small portion of moose meat in the lodge. The Weendigo looked around for something to eat, and being disappointed he took the lodge and threw it to the winds. He hardly seemed to notice the woman, for she was but a morsel for him. However, he grasped her by the waist. Her

140

cries and entreaties, with those of her son, had no effect—the monster tore out her entrails, and taking her body at one mouthful, started off without noticing the boy, probably thinking is was not worth his while to take half a mouthful.

When the hunter returned from the forest, he did not know what to think. His lodge was gone, and he saw his son sitting near the spot where it had stood, shedding tears. On a nearer approach he saw a few remains of his wife, and his son related all the circumstances of her death. The man blackened his face and vowed in his heart he would have revenge. He built another lodge, and collecting the remains of his wife, placed them in the hollow part of a dry tree. He left his boy to take care of the lodge while he was absent, hunting, and would roam about from place to place, trying to forget his misfortune. He made a bow and arrows for his son, and did every thing in his power to please him.

One day, while he was absent, his son shot his arrows out, through the top of the lodge, but when he went out to look for them he could not find them. His father made him some more, and when he was again left alone, he shot one of them out, but although he paid particular attention to the spot where it fell, he could not find it. He shot another, and immediately ran out of the lodge to see where it fell. He was surprised to see a beautiful boy, just in the act of taking it up, and running with it toward a large tree, where he disappeared. He followed, and having come to the tree, he beheld the face of the boy, looking out through an opening in the hollow part. Nha-ha (oh dear,) he said, my friend, come out and play with me. And he urged him till he consented. They played and shot their arrows by turns. Suddenly the younger boy said, "your father is coming. We must stop. Promise me that you will not tell him." The elder promised, and the other disappeared in the tree. The elder boy then went home, and when his father returned from the chase, sat demurely by the fire. In the course of the evening he asked his father to make him a new bow. To an inquiry of his father as to the use he meant to make of two bows, he replied, that one might break, or get lost; he then consented.

Next day the hunter made ready for the chase as usual. The boy said, "Father, try and hunt all day, and see what you can kill". As soon as he had gone, the boy called his friend, and they played and chased each other round the lodge. The man was returning and came to a rising piece of ground, when he heard his son laughing and making a noise, but the sounds appeared as if they arose from *two* persons playing. At the same instant the young boy of the tree stopped, and after saying, "your father is coming", ran off to the tree,

which stood near the lodge. The hunter, on entering found his son sitting near the fire, very quiet, but he was much surprised to see all the articles of the lodge lying in various directions. "Why, my son", said he, "you must play *very* hard, every day, and what do you do, all alone to throw about all our things in this manner, and cause the ashes to spread about the lodge". The boy again made excuse. "Father", said he, "I play in *this* manner—I chase and drag my coat around the lodge, and that is the reason you see ashes spread about". The hunter was not satisfied until he saw his son play with the coat, which he did so adroitly as to deceive him. Next day the boy repeated his request that the father would be absent all day, and see if he could not kill *two* deer. He thought it strange for his son to make such a request, and rather suspected something. He, however, went into the forest, and when out of sight, his son went for his young companion to the tree, and they resumed their sports. The father, on coming home at evening, when he reached the rising ground, which almost overlooked the lodge, heard again the sounds of laughing and playing, and could not be mistaken; he was now certain there were two voices. The boy from the tree had barely time to escape, when he entered and found his son, sitting as usual, near the fire. "My son", said he, "you must be very foolish, when alone, to play so. But tell me—I heard two voices I am certain", and he looked closely on the prints of the footsteps in the ashes. "True", he said, "here is the print of a foot that is smaller than my son's", which satisfied him that his suspicions were well founded, and that some very young person had played with his son. The boy, at this time, thought best to tell his father all that had been done. "Why, father", said he, "I found a boy in the hollow of the tree, near the lodge, where you put my mother's bones". Strange thoughts came over the man; he thought that this little boy might have been created from the remains of his deceased wife. But as Indians are generally fearful of disturbing the dead, he did not dare to go near the place where he had placed her remains. He thought best to tell his son, and make him promise, that he would entice his friend to a dead tree, that was near their lodge, by telling him that they could kill many flying squirrels by setting fire to it. He said he would conceal himself near by, and take the boy. Next day the hunter went into the woods, and his son went and insisted on his friend's going with him to kill the squirrels. He objected that his father was near, but was, at length, persuaded to go, and, after they had set fire to the tree, and while they were busy in killing the squirrels, the father suddenly made his appearance and clasped the boy in his arms. He cried out, Kago! Kago! (don't, don't) you will tear my clothes—which appeared to have been made of a fine transparent skin. The father now knew that it was the Great Spirit who had thus miraculously raised him a son from the remains of his wife; and he felt persuaded that the boy would aid him in his revenge on the Weendigoes. The hunter was now more reconciled to the loss of his wife, and spent as much time as he could spare from the chase, in attending to his sons. But what was very remarkable, both his sons retained their low stature, although they were well formed and beautiful.

One day he advised his sons not to go near a certain lake, which, he said, was inhabited by foul birds, who were vicious and dangerous. In the course of one of their rambles, the boys had wandered near it, and they came out and stood on its banks. They saw, on one side, a mountain, rising precipitously from the water, and reaching apparently to the sky. The youngest spoke and said, "I see no harm in climbing the rock to see what is to be discovered on its top". They ascended, and had got up, with difficulty, half way, when the rumbling noise of thunder was heard, and lightning began to play near them. But they were undaunted, and reached the top, where they beheld an enormous bird's nest, and in it two very large young birds. Although they had only the soft down, as yet, on their bodies, they appeared to be monsters, and when the young men put a stick near their eyes, which they opened and shut very quick, the flashes they emitted broke the stick in pieces. They, however, took the young birds, and with great difficulty reached the lodge with them. When their father came home, they told him what fine birds they had, and requested him to tame them, and bring them up as pets, "for", said they, "when we took them we intended them for you". They told him where they had procured them. The father was now convinced that both his sons were gifted with supernatural powers.

One day, after musing for a long time, he told his sons that his time was come, and that he should have to follow his forefathers to the land of the west. "But," he continued, "before I leave this earth, my sons, listen to my advice." He proceeded to speak to them, and when he had done, the youngest said, "Father, you must remember the Weendigoes, and the misery they brought on you. You will now leave earth, with your two feathered favourites; but first we will feed them with the flesh of the mishegenabig." They did so, and their father departed amid thunder and lightnings, for the two birds were the offspring of thunder. He fixed his residence as directed by the Great Manito in the sky toward the north, and he retains his name to the present day, which is, The Thunder commencing in the north, and going south.

The racoon and crawfish

The Racoon searches the margins of streams for shell-fish, where he is generally sure of finding the as-shog-aish-i, or crawfish. Indian story says, that the enmity between these two species, and the consequent wariness of each for the other, was such, that the poor racoon, with all his stealthiness, was at last put to great straits for a meal. The crawfish would no longer venture near the shore, and the racoon was on the point of starvation. At length he fixed on this expedient to decoy his enemy.

Knowing the crawfish to feed on worms, he procured a quantity of old rotten wood (filled with these worms) and stuffing it in his mouth and ears, and powdering it over his body, he lay down by the water's edge, to induce the belief that he was dead.

An old crawfish came out warily from the water, and crawled around and over his apparently deceased enemy. He rejoiced to find an end put to his murderous career, and cried out to his fellows, "Come up my brothers and sisters, Aissibun (the Racoon) is dead, come up and eat him." When a great multitude had gathered around, the racoon suddenly sprung up, and set to killing and devouring them in such a way that not one was left alive.

While he was still engaged with the broken limbs, a little female crawfish, carrying her infant sister on her back, came up, seeking her relations. Finding they had all been devoured by the Racoon, she resolved not to survive the destruction of her kindred, but went boldly up to the enemy and said, "Here, Aissibun, you behold me and my little sister. We are all alone. You have eaten up our parents, and all our friends, eat us too." And she continued plaintively singing her chant.

The Racoon felt reproached by this act of courage and magnanimity. "No," said he, "I have banqueted on the largest and the fattest,—I will not dishonour myself by such little prey."

At this moment Manabozha happened to pass by seeing how things were. "Tyau!" said he to the Racoon, "thou are a thief and an unmerciful dog. Get thee up into trees, lest I change thee into one of these same worm-fish, for thou wast thyself originally a shell, and bearest in thy name the influence of my transforming hand."

He then took up the little supplicant crawfish and her infant sister and cast them into the stream. "There," said he, "you may dwell. Hide yourselves under the stones, and hereafter you shall be playthings for little children."

The powder
or the Storm-fool

The vernal equinox in America, north of the 44° of north latitude, generally takes place while the ground is covered with snow, and winter still wears a polar aspect. Storms of wind and light drifting snow, expressively called *poudre* by the French of the upper Lakes, fill the atmosphere, and render it impossible to distinguish objects at a short distance. The fine powdery flakes of snow are driven into the smallest crannies of buildings and fixtures, and seem to be endowed with a subtle power of insinuation, which renders northern joinerwork but a poor defence. It is not uncommon for the sleeper on waking up in the morning, to find heaps of snow, where he had supposed himself quite secure on lying down.

Such seasons are, almost invariably, times of scarcity and hunger with the Indians, for the light snows have buried up the traps of the hunters, and the fishermen are deterred from exercising their customary skill in decoying fish through the ice. They are often reduced to the greatest straits, and compelled to exercise their utmost ingenuity to keep their children from starving. Abstinence, on the part of the elder members of the family, is regarded both as a duty and a merit. Every effort is made to satisfy the importunity of the little ones for food, and if there be a story-teller in the lodge, he is sure to draw upon his cabin lore, to amuse their minds, and beguile the time.

In these storms, when each inmate of the lodge has his *conaus*, or wrapper, tightly drawn around him, and all are cowering around the cabin fire, should some sudden puff of wind drive a volume of light snow into the lodge, it would scarcely happen, but that some one of the group would cry out "Ah, Pauppukeewiss is now gathering his harvest," an expression which has the effect to put them all into good humour.

Pauppukeewiss, was a crazy brain, who played many queer tricks, but took care, nevertheless, to supply his family and children with food. But, in this, he was not always successful. Many winters have passed since he was overtaken; at this very season of the year, with great want, and he, with his whole family, was on the point of starvation. Every resource seemed to have failed. The snow was so deep, and the storm continued so long, that he could not even find a partridge or a hare. And his usual resource of fish had entirely failed. His lodge stood in a point of woods, not far back from the shores of the Gitchiguma, or great water, where the autumnal storms had piled up the ice into high pinnacles, resembling castles.

"I will go," said he to his family one morning, "to these castles, and solicit the pity of the spirits, who inhabit them, for I know that they are the residence of some of the spirits of Kabiboonoka. He did so, and found that his petition was not disregarded. They told him to fill his mushkemoots, or sacks, with the ice and snow, and pass on toward his lodge, without looking back, until he came to a certain hill. He must then drop his sacks, and leave them till morning, when he would find them filled with fish.

They cautioned him, that he must by no means look back, although he would hear a great many voices crying out to him, in abusive terms, for these voices were nothing but the wind playing through the branches of the trees. He faithfully obeyed the injunction, although he found it hard to avoid turning round, to see who was calling out to him. And when he visited his sacks in the morning, he found them filled with fish.

It chanced that Manabozho visited him on the morning that he brought home the sacks of fish. He was invited to partake of a feast, which Pauppukeewiss ordered to be prepared for him. While they were eating, Manabozho could not help asking him, by what means he had procured such an abundance of food, at a time when they were all in a state of starvation.

Pauppukeewiss frankly told him the secret, and repeated the precautions which were necessary to ensure success. Manabozho determined to profit by his information, and as soon as he could, he set out to visit the icy castles. All things happened as he had been told. The spirits seemed propitious, and told him to fill and carry. He accordingly filled his sacks with ice and snow, and proceeded rapidly toward the hill of transmutation. But as he ran he heard voices calling out behind him, "thief!" "thief! He has stolen fish from Kabiboo-noka," cried one. "Mukumik! mukumik! Take it away! Take it away!" cried another.

In fine his ears were so assailed by all manner of opprobrious terms, that he could not avoid turning his head, to see who it was that thus abused him. But his curiosity dissolved the charm. When he came to visit his bags next morning, he found them filled with ice and snow.

In consequence, he is condemned every year, during the month of March, to run over the hills, with Pappukeewiss following him, with the cries of mukumik! mukumik!

Git-Chee-Gau
Zinee or the trance

Git-Chee-Gau-Zinee, after a few days' illness, suddenly expired in the presence of his friends, by whom he was beloved and lamented. He had been an expert hunter, and left, among other things, a fine gun, which he had requested might be buried with his body. There were some who thought his death a suspension and not an extinction of the animal functions, and that he would again be restored. His widow was among the number, and she carefully watched the body for the space of four days. She thought thay by laying her hand upon his breast she could discover remaining indications of vitality. Twenty-four hours had elapsed, and nearly every vestige of hope had departed, when the man came to life. He gave the following narration to his friends:

"After death, my Jeebi travelled in the broad road of the dead toward the happy land, which is the Indian paradise. I passed on many days without meeting with any thing of an extraordinary nature. At length I began to suffer for the want of food. I reached the summit of an elevation. My eyes caught the glimpse of the city of the dead. But it appeared to be distant, and the intervening space, partly veiled in silvery mists, was spangled with glittering lakes and streams. At this spot I came in sight of numerous herds of stately deer, moose, and other animals, which walked bear my path, and appeared to have lost their natural timidity. But having no gun I was unable to kill them. I thought of the request I had made to my friends, to put my gun in my grave, and resolved to go back and seek for it. "I found I had the free use of my limbs and faculties and I had no sooner made this resolution, than I turned back. But I now beheld an immense number of men, women, and children, travelling toward the city of the dead, every one of whom I had to face in going back. I saw, in this throng, persons of every age, from the little infant—the sweet and lovely *Penaisee* (the term of endearment for a young son), to the feeble gray-headed man, stooping with the weight of years. All whom I met, however, were heavily laden with implements, guns, pipes, kettles, meats, and other articles. One man stopped me and complained of the great burdens he had to carry. He offered me his gun, which I however refused, having made up my mind to procure my own. Another offered me a kettle.

"After encoutering this throng for two days and nights, I came to the place where I had died. But I could see nothing but a great fire, the flames of which rose up before me, and spread around me. Whichever way I turned to avoid them, the flames still barred my advance. I was in the utmost perplexity, and knew not what to do. At length I determined to make a desperate leap, thinking my friends were on the other side, and in this effort, I awoke from my trance." Here the chief paused, and after a few moments concluded his story with the following admonitory remarks: "My chiefs and friends," said he, "I will tell you of one practice, in which our forefathers have been wrong. They have been accustomed to deposit too many things with the dead. These implements are burthensome to them. It requires a longer time for them to reach the peace of repose, and almost every one I have conversed with, complained bitterly to me of the evil. It would be wiser to put such things only, in the grave, as the deceased was particularly attached to, or made a formal request to have deposited with him. If he has been successful in the chase, and has abundance of things in his lodge, it would be better that they should remain for his family. Advice which comes in this pleasing form of story and allegory, can give offence to no one. And it is probably the mode which the northern Indians have employed, from the earliest times, to rebuke faults and instil instruction. The old men, upon whom the duty of giving advice uniformly falls, may have found this the most efficacious means of moulding opinion and forming character.

Osseo or the son of the Evening Star

There once lived an Indian in the north, who had ten daughters, all of whom grew up to womanhood. They were noted for their beauty, but especially Oweenee, the youngest, who was very independent in her way of thinking. She was a great admirer of romantic places, and paid very little attention to the numerous young men who came to her father's lodge for the purpose of seeing her. Her elder sisters were all solicited in marriage from their parents, and one after another, went off to dwell in the lodges of their husbands, or mothers-in-law, but she would listen to no proposals of the kind. At last she married an old man called Osseo, who was scarcely able to walk, and was too poor to have things like others. They jeered and laughed at her, on all sides, but she seemed to be quite happy, and said to them, "It is my choice, and you will see in the end, who has acted the wisest." Soon after, the sisters and their husbands and their parents were all invited to a feast, and as they walked along the path, they could not help pitying their young and handsome sister, who had such an unsuitable mate. Osseo often stopped and gazed upwards, but they could perceive nothing in the direction he looked, unless it was the faint glimmering of the evening star. They heard him muttering to himself as they went along, and one of the elder sisters caught the words, "Sho-wain-ne-me-shin nosa" (Pity me, my father). "Poor old man,", said she, "he is talking to his father, what a pity it is, that he would not fall and break his neck, that our sister might have a handsome young husband." Presently they passed a large hollow log, lying with one end toward the path. The moment Osseo, who was of the turtle totem, came to it, he stopped short, uttered a loud and peculiar yell, and then dashing into one end of the log, he came out at the other, a most beautiful young man, and springing back to the road, he led off the party with steps as light as the reindeer. But on turning round to look for his wife, behold, she had been changed into an old, decrepit woman, who was bent almost double, and walked with a cane. The husband, however, treated her very kindly, as she had done him during the time of his enchantment, and constantly addressed her by the term of ne-ne-moosh-a, or my sweetheart.

When they came to the hunter's lodge with whom they were to feast, they found the feast ready prepared, and as soon as their entertainer had finished his harangue, (in which he told them his feasting was in honour of the Evening, or Woman's Star,) they began to partake of the portion dealt out, according to age and character, to each one. The food was very delicious, and they were all happy but Osseo, who, looked at his wife and then gazed upward, as if he was looking into the substance of the sky. Sounds were soon heard, as if from far-off voices in the air, and they became plainer and plainer, tiill he could clearly distinguish some of the words.

"My son—my son," said the voice, "I have seen your afflictions and pity your wants. I come to call you away from a scene that is stained with blood and tears. The earth is full of sorrows. Giants and sorcerers, the enemies of mankind, walk abroad in it, and are scattered throughout its length. Every night they are lifting their voices to the Power of Evil, and every day they make themselves busy in casting evil in the hunter's path. You have long been their victim, but shall be their victim no more. The spell you were under is broken. Your evil genius is overcome. I have cast him down by my superior strength, and it is this strength I now exert for your happiness. Ascend, my son—ascend into the skies, and partake of the feast I have prepared for you in the stars, and bring with you those you love.

"The food set before you is enchanted and blessed. Fear not to partake of it. It is endowed with magic power to give immortality to mortals, and to

156

change men to spirits. Your bowls and kettles shall be no longer wood and earth. The one shall become silver, and the other wampum. They shall shine like fire, and glisten like the most beautiful scarlet. Every female shall also change her state and looks, and no longer be doomed to laborious tasks. She shall put on the beauty of the starlight, and become a shining bird of the air, clothed with shining feathers. She shall dance and not work—she shall sing and not cry."

"My beams," continued the voice, "shine faintly on your lodge, but they have a power to transform it into the lightness of the skies, and decorate it with the colours of the clouds. Come, Osseo, my son, and dwell no longer on earth. Think strongly on my words, and look steadfastly at my beams. My power is now at its height. Doubt not—delay not. It is the voice of the Spirit of the stars that calls you away to happiness and celestial rest."

The words were intelligible to Osseo, but his companions thought them some far-off sounds of music, or birds singing in the woods. Very soon the lodge began to shake and tremble, and they felt it rising into the air. It was too late to run out, for they were already as high as the tops of the trees. Osseo looked around him as the lodge passed through the topmost boughs, and behold! their wooden dishes were changed into shells of a scarlet colour, the poles of the lodge to glittering wires of silver, and the bark that covered them into the gorgeous wings of insects. A moment more, and his brothers and sisters, and their parents and friends, were transformed into birds, of various plumage. Some were jays, some partridges and pigeons, and others gay singing birds, who hopped about displaying their glittering feathers, and singing their songs. But Oweenee still kept her earthly garb, and exhibited all the indications of extreme age. He again cast his eyes in the direction of the clouds, and uttered that peculiar yell, which had given him the victory at the hollow log. In a moment the youth and beauty of his wife returned; her dingy garments assumed the shining appearance of green silk, and her cane was changed into a silver feather. The lodge again shook and trembled, for they were now passing through the uppermost clouds, and they immediately after found themselves in the Evening Star, the residence of Osseo's father.

"My son," said the old man, "hang that cage of birds, which you have brought along in your hand, at the door, and I will inform you why you and your wife have been sent for." Osseo obeyed the directions, and then took his seat in the lodge. "Pity was shown to you," resumed the king of the star, "on

account of the contempt of your wife's sister, who laughed at her ill fortune, and ridiculed you while you were under the power of that wicked spirit, whom you overcame at the log. That spirit lives in the next lodge, being a small star you see on the left of mine, and he has always felt envious of my family, because we had greater power than he had, and especially on account of our having had the care committed to us of the female world. He failed in several attempts to destroy your brothers-in-law and sisters-in-law, but succeeded at last in transforming yourself and your wife into decrepit old persons. You must be careful and not let the light of his beams fall on you, while you are here, for therein is the power of his enchantment; a ray of light is the bow and arrows he uses."

Osseo lived happy and contented in the parental lodge, and in due time his wife presented him with a son, who grew up rapidly, and was the image of his father. He was very quick and ready in learning every thing that was done in his grandfather's dominions, but he wished also to learn the art of hunting, for he had heard that this was a favourite pursuit below. To gratify him his father made him a bow and arrows, and he then let the birds out of the cage that he might practise in shooting. He soon became expert, and the very first day brought down a bird, but when he went to pick it up, to his amazement, it was a beautiful young woman with the arrow sticking in her breast. It was one of his younger *aunts*. The moment her blood fell upon the surface of that pure and spotless planet, the charm was dissolved. The boy immediately found himself sinking, but was partly upheld, by something like wings, till he passed through the lower clouds, and he then suddenly dropped upon a high, romantic island in a large lake. He was pleased on looking up, to see all his aunts and uncles following him in the form of birds, and he soon discovered the silver lodge, with his father and mother, descending with its waving barks looking like so many insects' gilded wings. It rested on the highest cliffs of the island, and here they fixed their residence. They all resumed their natural *shapes*, but were diminished to the *size* of fairies, and as a mark of homage to the King of the Evening Star, they never failed, on every pleasant evening, during the summer season, to join hands, and dance upon the top of the rocks. These rocks were quickly observed by the Indians to be covered, in moonlight evenings, with a larger sort of Puk Wudj Ininees, or little men, and were called Mish-in-e-mok-in-ok-ong, or turtle spirits, and the island is named from them to this day. (Michilimackinac, the term alluded to, is the original French orthography of Mish en I mok in ong, the *local* form (sing, and plu.), of Turtle Spirits). Their shining lodge can be seen in the summer evenings when the moon shines strongly on the pinnacles or the rocks, and the fishermen, who go near those high cliffs at night, have even heard the voices of the happy little dancers.

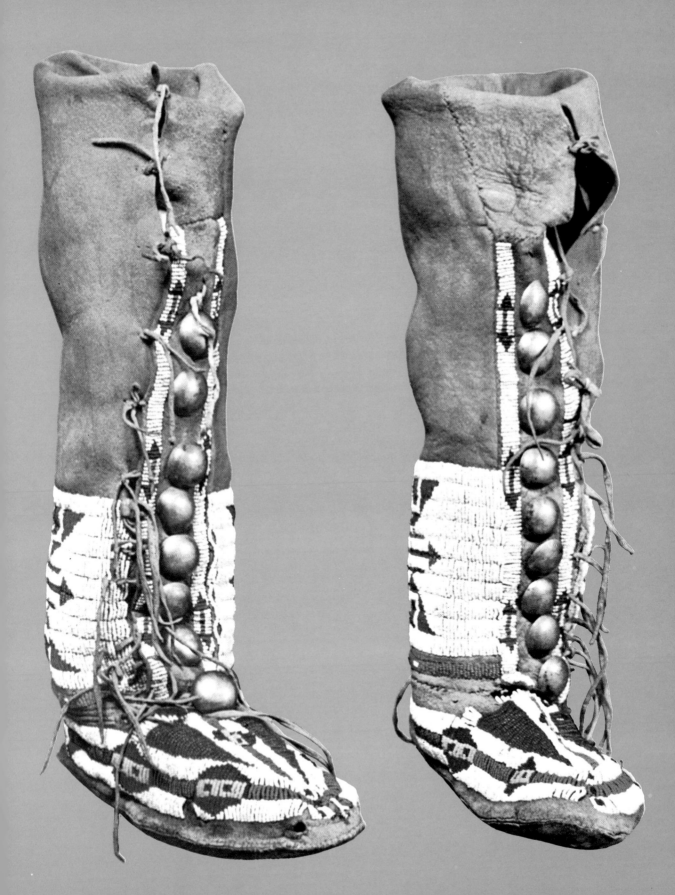

Kwasind or the fearfully strong man

Pauwating was a village where the young men amused themselves very much in ancient times, in sports and ball-playing.

One day as they were engaged in their sports, one of the strongest and most active, at the moment he was about to succeed in a trial of lifting, slipped and fell upon his back. "Ha! ha! ha!" cried the lookers on, "you will never rival Kwasind." He was deeply mortified, and when the sport was over, these words came to his mind. He could not recollect any man of this name. He thought he would ask the old man, the story-teller of the village, the next time he came to the lodge. The opportunity soon occurred.

"My grandfather," said he, "who was Kwasind? I am very anxious to know what he could do."

Kwasind, the old man replied, was a listless idle boy. He would not play when the other boys played, and his parents could never get him to do any kind of labour. He was always making excuses. His parents took notice, however, that he fasted for days together, but they could not learn what spirit he supplicated, or had chosen as the guardian spirit to attend him through life.

He was so inattentive to his parents' requests, that he, at last, became a subject of reproach.

"Ah," said his mother to him one day, "is there any young man of your age, in all the village, who does so little for his parents? You neither hunt nor fish. You take no interest in any thing, whether labour or amusement, which engages the attention of your equals in years. I have often set my nets (nets are set in winter, in high northern latitudes, through orifices cut in the ice) in the coldest days of winter, without any assistance from you. And I have taken them up again, while you remained inactive at the lodge fire. Are you not ashamed of such idleness? Go, I bid you, and wring out that net, which I have just taken from the water."

Kwasind saw that there was a determination to make him obey. He did not therefore make any excuses, but went out and took up the net. He carefully folded it, doubled and redoubled it, forming it into a roll, and then with an easy twist of his hands wrung it short off, with as much ease as if every twine had been a thin brittle fibre. Here, they at once saw, the secret of his reluctance. He possessed supernatural strength.

After this, the young men were playing one day on the plain, where there was lying one of those large, heavy, black pieces of rock, which Manabozho is said to have cast at his father. Kwasind took it up with much ease, and threw it into the river. After this, he accompanied his father on a hunting excursion into a remote forest. They came to a place where the wind had thrown a great many trees into a narrow pass. "We must go the other way," said the old man, "it is impossible to get the burdens through this place." He sat down to rest himself, took out his smoking apparatus, and gave a short time to reflection. When he had finished, Kwasind had lifted away the largest pine trees, and pulled them out of the path.

Sailing one day in his canoe, Kwasind saw a large furred animal, which he immediately recognised to be the king of beavers. He plunged into the water in pursuit of it. His companions were in the greatest astonishment and alarm, supposing he would perish. He often dove down and remained a long time under water, pursuing the animal from island to island; and at last returned with the kingly prize. After this, his fame spread far and wide, and no hunter would presume to compete with him.

He performed so many feats of strength and skill, that he excited the envy of the Puck-wudj In-in-ee-sug, or fairies, who conspired against his life.

162

"For," said they, "if this man is suffered to go on, in his career of strength and exploits, we shall presently have no work to perform. Our agency in the affairs of men must cease. He will undermine our power, and drive us, at last, into the water, where we must all perish, or be devoured by the wicked Neebanawbaig (a kind of water spirits).

The strength of Kwasind was all concentrated in the crown of his head. This was, at the same time, the only vulnerable part of his body; and there was but one species of weapon which could be successfully employed in making any impression upon it. The fairies carefully hunted through the woods to find this weapon. It was the burr or seed vessel of the white pine. They gathered a quantity of this article, and waylaid Kwasind at a point on the river, where the red rocks jut into the water, forming rude castles—a point which he was accustomed to pass in his canoe. They waited a long time, making merry upon these rocks, for it was a highly romantic spot. At last the wished-for object appeared, Kwasind came floating calmly down the stream, on the afternoon of a summer's day, languid with the heat of the weather, and almost asleep. When his canoe came directly beneath the cliff, the tallest and stoutest fairy began the attack. Others followed his example. It was a long time before they could hit the vulnerable part, but success at length crowned their efforts, and Kwasind sunk, never to rise more.

Ever since this victory, the Puck Wudj Ininee have made that point of rock a favourite resort. The hunters often hear them laugh, and see their little plumes shake as they pass this scene on light summer evenings.

"My son," continued the old man, "take care that you do not imitate the faults of Kwasind. If he had not so often exerted his strength merely for the sake of *boasting*, he would not, perhaps, have made the fairies feel jealous of him. It is better to use the strength you have, in a quiet useful way, than to sigh after the possession of a giant's power. For if you run, or wrestle, or jump, or fire at a mark, only as well as your equals in years, nobody will envy you. But if you would needs be a Kwasind, you must expect a Kwasind's fate."

The spirit of evil
and the spirit of good

In a beautiful portion of the country, which was part forest and part prairie, there lived a bloodthirsty Manito in the guise of an Indian, who made use of all his arts to decoy men into his power for the purpose of killing them. Although the country yielded an abundance of game, and every other production to satisfy his wants, yet it was the study of his life to destroy human beings, and subsist upon their blood. The country had once been thickly populated, but he had thinned it off by his wickedness, and his lodge was surrounded by the bleached bones of his victims.

The secret of his success lay in his great speed. He had the power to assume the shape of any quadruped, and it was his custom to challenge persons to run with him. He had a beaten path on which he ran, leading around a large lake, and he always ran around this circle, so that the starting and winning point were the same. At this point stood a post, having a sharp and shining knife tied to it, and whoever lost the race lost his life. The winner immediately took up the knife and cut off his competitor's head. No man was ever known to beat this evil Manito in the race, although he ran every day; for whenever he was pressed hard, he changed himself into a fox, wolf, or deer, or other swift-footed animal, and thus left his competitor behind.

The whole country was in dread of him, and yet, such was the folly and rashness of the young men, that they were continually running with him; for if they refused, he called them cowards, which was a taunt they could not bear. They would rather die than be called cowards. In other respects, the Manito had pleasing manners, and visited the lodges around the country, like others; but his secret object in these visits was to see whether the young boys were getting to be old enough to run with him, and he was careful to keep a watch upon their growth, and never failed to challenge them to run on his race ground. There was no family which had not lost some of its most active members in this way, and the Manito was execrated by all the Indian mothers in the country.

There lived near him a widow, whose husband and ten sons he had killed in this way, and she was now left with an only daughter and a son of ten or twelve years old, named Monedowa. She was very poor and feeble, and suffered so much for the want of food, that she would have been glad to die, had it not been for her daughter and her little son, who was not yet able to hunt. The Manito had already visited her lodge to see whether the boy was not sufficiently grown to challenge him. And the mother saw there was a great probability that he would be decoyed and killed as his father and brothers had been. Still, she hoped a better fate would attend him, and strove, in the best way she could, to instruct him in the maxims of a hunter's and a warrior's life. To the daughter she also taught all that could make her useful as a wife, and instructed her in the arts of working with porcupine quills on leather, and various other things, which the Indian females regard as accomplishments. She was also neat and tasteful in arranging her dress according to their customs, and possessing a tall and graceful person, she displayed her national costume to great advantage. She was kind and obedient to her mother, and never neglected to perform her appropriate domestic duties. Her mother's lodge stood on an elevation on the banks of a lake, which gave them a fine prospect of the country for many miles around, the interior of which was diversified with groves and prairies. It was in this quarter that they daily procured their fuel. One day the daughter had gone out to these open groves to pick up dry limbs for their fire, and while admiring the scenery, she strolled farther than usual, and was suddenly startled by the appearance of a young man near her. She would have fled, but was arrested by his pleasing smile, and by hearing herself addressed in her own language. The questions he asked were trivial, relating to her place of residence and family, and were answered with timidity. It could not be concealed, however; that they were mutually pleased with each other, and before parting, he asked her to get her mother's consent to their marriage. She returned home later than usual, but was too timid to say anything to her mother on the subject. The meetings, however, with her admirer on the borders of the prairie, were frequent, and he every time requested her to speak to her mother on the subject of their marriage, which, however, she could not muster the resolution to do. At last the widow suspected something of the kind, from the tardiness of her daughter in coming in, and from the scanty quantity of fuel she sometimes brought. In answer to inquiries, she revealed the circumstance of her meeting the young man, and of his request. After reflecting upon her lonely and destitute situation, the mother gave her consent. The daughter went with a light step to communicate the answer, which her lover heard with delight, and after saying that he would come to the lodge at sunset, they separated. He was punctual to his engagement, and came at the precise time, dressed out as a warrior with every customary decoration, and approached the lodge with a mild and pleasing, yet manly air and commanding step. On entering it, he spoke affectionately to his mother-in-law, whom he called (contrary to the usage,) Neejee, *or friend.* She directed him to sit down beside her daughter, and from this moment they were regarded as man and wife.

Early the following morning, he asked for the bow and arrows of those who had been slain by the Manito, and went out a hunting. As soon as he had got out of sight of the lodge, he transformed himself into a Peena, or partridge, and took his flight in the air. Where or how he procured his food, is unknown; but he returned at evening with the carcasses of two deer. This continued to be his daily practice, and it was not long before the scaffolds near the lodge were loaded with meat. It was observed, however, that he ate but little himself, and that of a peculiar kind of meat, which added to some other particulars, convinced the family of his mysterious character. In a few days his mother-in-law told him that the Manito would come to pay them a visit, to see how the young man prospered. He told her that he should be away that day purposely, but would return the moment the visiter left them. On the day named he flew upon a tall tree, overlooking the lodge, and took his stand there to observe the movement of the Manito. This wicked spirit soon appeared, and as he passed the scaffolds of meat, cast suspicious glances toward them. He had no sooner

167

entered the lodge, stopping first to look, before he went in, than he said—"Why, woman, who is it that is furnishing you meat so plentifully?" "No one," she answered, "but my son—he is just beginning to kill deer." "No, no," said he, "some one is living with you." "Kaween," (No indeed!) said the old woman, dissembling again, "You are only jesting on my destitute situation. Who do you think would come and trouble themselves about *me?*" "Very well," replied the Manito, "I will go; but on such a day, I will again visit you, and see who it is that furnishes the meat, and whether it is your son or not." He had no sooner left the lodge and got out of sight, than the son-in-law made his appearance with two more deer. On being told of the particulars of the visit, "Very well," said he, "I will be at home next time and see him." They remonstrated against this, telling him of his cruelties, and the barbarous murders he had committed. "No matter," said he, "if he invites me to the race ground, I will not be backward. The result will teach him to show pity on the vanquished, and not to trample on the widow, and those who are without fathers." When the day of the expected visit arrived, he told his wife to prepare certain pieces of meat, which he pointed out and handed to her, together with two or three buds of the birch-tree which he requested her to put in the pot; and he directed that nothing should be wanting to show the usual hospitality to their guest, although he knew that his only object was to kill him. He then dressed himself as a warrior, putting tints of red on his visage and dress, to show that he was prepared for either war or peace.

As soon as the Manito arrived, he eyed this, to him, strange warrior, but dissembled his feelings, and spoke laughingly to the old woman, saying, "Did I not tell you that some one was staying with you, for I knew your son was too young to hunt!" She turned it off by saying that she did not think it neccessary to tell him, as he was a Manito and knew before asking. He then conversed with the son-in-law on different topics, and finished by inviting him to the race ground, saying it was a manly amusement—that it would give him an opportunity of seeing other men, and he should himself be pleased to run with him. The young man said he knew nothing of running. "Why," he replied, "don't you see how old I look, while you are young and active. We must at least run to amuse others." "Be it so, then," replied the young man, "I will go in the morning." Pleased with his success, the Manito now wished to return, but he was pressed to remain and partake of the customary hospitalities, although he endeavoured to excuse himself. The meal was immediately spread. But one dish was used. The young man partook of it first, to show his guest that he need not fear to partake, and saying at the same time to him, "It is a feast, and as we seldom meet, we must eat all that is placed on the dish, as a mark of gratitude to the Great Spirit for permitting me to kill the animals, and for the pleasure of seeing you, and partaking of it with you." They ate and conversed until they had eaten nearly all, when the Manito took up the dish and drank the broth. On setting it down, he immediately turned his head and commenced coughing violently, having, as the young man expected, swallowed a grain of the birch tops, which had lodged in his windpipe. He coughed incessantly, and found his situation so unpleasant, that he had to leave, saying, as he quit the lodge, that he should expect the young man at the race ground in the morning.

Monedowa prepared himself early in the morning by oiling his limbs, and decorating himself so as to appear to advantage, and having procured leave for his brother to attend him, they repaired to the Manito's race ground. The Manito's lodge stood on an eminence, and a row of other lodges stood near it, and as soon as the young man and his companion came near it, the inmates cried out, "We are visited." At this cry he came out, and descended with them to the starting post on a plain. From this, the course could be seen, as it wound around the lake, and as soon as the people assembled, he began to speak of the race, then belted himself up, and pointed to the knife which hung on the post, and said it was to be used by the winner. "But before we start," said the old man, "I wish it to be understood, that when men run with me, I make a bet, and expect them to abide by it. Life against life." He then gave a yell, casting a triumphant glance on the piles of human bones that were scattered about the stake. "I am ready," replied the stranger, as he was called, (for no one knew the widow's son-in-law,) and they all admired the symmetry and beauty of his limbs, and the fine and bold air which he assumed before his grim antagonist. The shout was given, and they went off with surprising speed, and were soon out of sight. The old man began to show his power by changing himself into a fox, and passing the stranger with great ease, went leisurely along. Monedowa now exerted his magic powers by assuming the shape of a partridge, and lighting a distance ahead of his antagonist, resumed his former shape. When the Manito spied his opponent ahead, "Whoa! whoa!" he exclaimed involuntarily, "this is strange," and immediately changed himself into a wolf, and repassed him. As he went by, he heard a whistling noise in the Manito's throat. He again took flight as a partridge, ascending some distance into the

169

air, and then suddenly coming down with great velocity, as partridges do, lit in the path far ahead. As he passed the wolf, he addressed him thus: "My friend, is this the extent of your speed." The Manito began to have strong forebodings, for, on looking ahead, he saw the stranger in his natural shape, running along very leisurely. He then assumed alternately the shapes of various animals noted for speed. He again passed the stranger in the shape of a reindeer. They had now got round the circle of the lake, and were approaching the point of starting, when the stranger again took his flight as a partridge, and lit some distance in advance. To overtake him, the Manito at last assumed the shape of a buffalo, and again got ahead; but it appears this was the last form he could assume, and it was that, in which he had most commonly conquered. The stranger again took his flight as a partridge, and in the act of passing his competitor saw his tongue hanging out from fatigue. "My friend," said he, "is this all your speed?" The Manito answered not. The stranger had now got within a flight of the winning post, when the fiend had nearly caught up to him. "Bakah! bakah! neejee," he vociferated. "Stop, my friend, I wish to talk to you," for he felt that he should be defeated and lose his life, and it was his purpose to beg for it. The stranger laughed, as he replied, "I will speak to you at the starting post. When men run with me, I make a bet, and expect them to abide by it. Life against life." And immediately taking his flight, alighted so near to the goal, that he could easily reach it in his natural form. The Manito saw the movement, and was paralyzed. The people at the stake shouted. The stranger ran with his natural speed, his limbs displaying to great advantage, and the war eagle's feathers waving on his head. The shouts were redoubled, hope added to his speed, and amid the din, he leaped to the post, and grasping the shining blade, stood ready to despatch his adversary the moment of his arrival. The Manito came, with fear and cowardice depicted in his face. "My friend," said he, "spare my life," and then added in a low voice, as if he did not wish others to hear it, "give me to live," and began to move off, as if the request was granted. "As you have done to others," replied the noble youth, "so shall it be done to you;" and his bleeding head rolled down the sloping hill. The spectators then drew their knives, and cut his body into numberless pieces. The conqueror then asked to be led to the Manito's lodge, the interior of which had never been seen. Few had ever dared even to ascend the eminence on which it stood. On entering, they saw that it consisted of several apartments. The first was arranged and furnished as Indian lodges usually are. But horror struck upon his mind as they entered the second,—it was entirely surrounded by a wall of human skulls and bones, with pieces of human flesh scattered about. Upon a scaffold, the dead bodies of two human beings were hanging, cut open, for the purpose of drying the flesh. The third apartment had its sides beautifully decorated, but horrid to behold, two monsters in the form of black snakes, lay coiled up, one on each side of the lodge. It appears that one of them was the wife, and the other the child of the Manito. They were Mishegenabikoes, or Devils. This was also the natural shape of the Manito, but he had assumed the human form only to deceive. The orifice by which they had originally come out of the earth was closed, and escape for them was impossible. The magic knife still glittered in the stranger's hand, and without a moment's delay, he severed both their heads. He then commanded the people to bring together combustibles, which they set fire to, and consumed their remains. When the fire reached their carcasses, a dark smoke ascended from the lodge, and the hideous forms of fiery serpents were seen curling amid the flames.

The mysterious stranger, who had thus proved their deliverer, then commanded them to bring together all the human bones scattered around, and after making due preparations, he chose three magic arrows, and shooting the first into the air, cried, "Arise!" He then shot the second, repeating the cry, and immediately shot the third, uttering aloud, "Arise!" And the bones arose, and stood up covered with flesh, in their natural forms. And they instantly raised a loud and joyous shout of thanks to their deliverer.

The Genius of Benevolence (for such we must now regard him), motioned to all the people to keep silence, and addressed them as follows; "My friends, the Great Spirit who lives above the skies, seeing the cruelties of the Manito I have destroyed, was moved with pity for you, and determined to rid the earth of such a monster. I am the creation of His thinking mind, and therein first appeared, and he gave me such power, that when the word was spoken, it was done. When I wished to have the swiftness of a bird, I flew, and whatever power I wanted was given me. You are witnesses of it, and have seen the Mudjee Monedo killed and burned, and the bones of his victims get up and shout. This is as nothing with Him. It was done to restore your friends. And this will be the way when the earth has an end, for all people will arise again, and friends unite in going to the happy hunting grounds, when they will see who directs all things. My stay with you will be short, for I must return whence I came. During this brief time, I will, however, instruct you, and teach you to live happy".

The whole multitude then followed him to the widow's lodge, where he taught them what to do. They built their lodges around him, forming a very large town. They dug up the earth and planted—they built large houses, and learned many new arts, and were happy. Not as it is now—for all the Indians have forgotten it. Having done this, he ascended into the clouds, leaving his wife the future mother of a son, to whom he referred the people assembled to witness his departure, for subsequent counsel.

Weeng

Sleep is personified by the Algic race, under the name of Weeng. But the power of the Indian Morpheus is executed in a peculiar manner, and by a novel agency. Weeng seldom acts directly in inducing sleep, but he exercises dominion over hosts of gnome-like beings, who are everywhere present, and are constantly on the alert. These beings are invisible to common eyes. Each one is armed with a tiny puggamaugon, or club, and when he observes a person sitting or reclining under circumstances favourable to sleep, he nimbly climbs upon his forehead and inflicts a blow. The first blow only creates drowsiness, the second makes the person lethargic, so that he occasionally closes his eyelids, the third produces sound sleep. It is the constant duty of these little emissaries to put every one to sleep whom they encounter—men, women, and children. And they are found secreted around the bed, or on small protuberances of the bark of the Indian lodges. They hide themselves in the Gush-keepitaugun, or smoking pouch of the hunter, and when he sits down to light his pipe in the woods, are ready to fly out and exert their sleep-compelling power. If they succeed, the game is suffered to pass, and the hunter obliged to return to his lodge without a reward.

In general, however, they are represented to possess friendly dispositions, seeking constantly to restore vigour and elasticity to the exhausted body. But being without judgment, their power is sometimes exerted at the hazard of reputation, or even life. Sleep may be induced in a person carelessly floating in his canoe, above a fall; or in a war party, on the borders of an enemy's country; or in a female, without the protection of the lodge circle. Although their peculiar season of action is in the night, they are also alert during the day.

While the forms of these gnomes are believed to be those of *ininees*, little or fairy men, the figure of Weeng himself is unknown, and it is not certain that he has ever been seen. Most of what is known on this subject is derived from Iagoo, who related that, going out one day with his dogs to hunt, he passed through a wide range of thicket, where he lost his dogs. He became much alarmed, for they were faithful animals, and he was greatly attached to them. He called out, and made every exertion to recover them in vain. At length he came to a spot where he found them asleep, having incautiously run near the residence of Weeng. After great exertions he aroused them, but not without having felt the power of somnolency himself. As he cast up his eyes from the place where the dogs were lying, he saw the Spirit of Sleep sitting upon a branch of a tree. He was in the shape of a giant insect, or *monetoas*, with many wings from his back, which made a low deep murmuring sound, like distant falling water. But Iagoo himself being a very great liar and braggart, little credit was given to his narration.

Weeng is not only the dispenser of sleep, but, it seems, he is also the author of dullness, which renders the word susceptible of an ironical use. If an orator fails, he is said to be struck by Weeng. If a warrior *lingers*, he has ventured too near the sleepy god. If children begin to nod or yawn, the Indian mother looks up smilingly, and says, "they have been struck by Weeng," and puts them to bed.

The pigeon hawk
and tortoise

The pigeon hawk bantered the tortoise for a race, but the tortoise declined it, unless he would consent to run several days' journey. The hawk very quickly consented, and they immediately set out.

The tortoise knew, that if he obtained the victory it must be by great diligence, so he went down into the earth, and taking a straight line, stopped for nothing.

The hawk, on the contrary, knowing that he could easily beat his competitor, kept carelessly flying this way and that way in the air, stopping now to visit one, and then another, till so much time had been lost, that when he came in sight of the winning point, the tortoise had just come up out of the earth, and gained the prize.

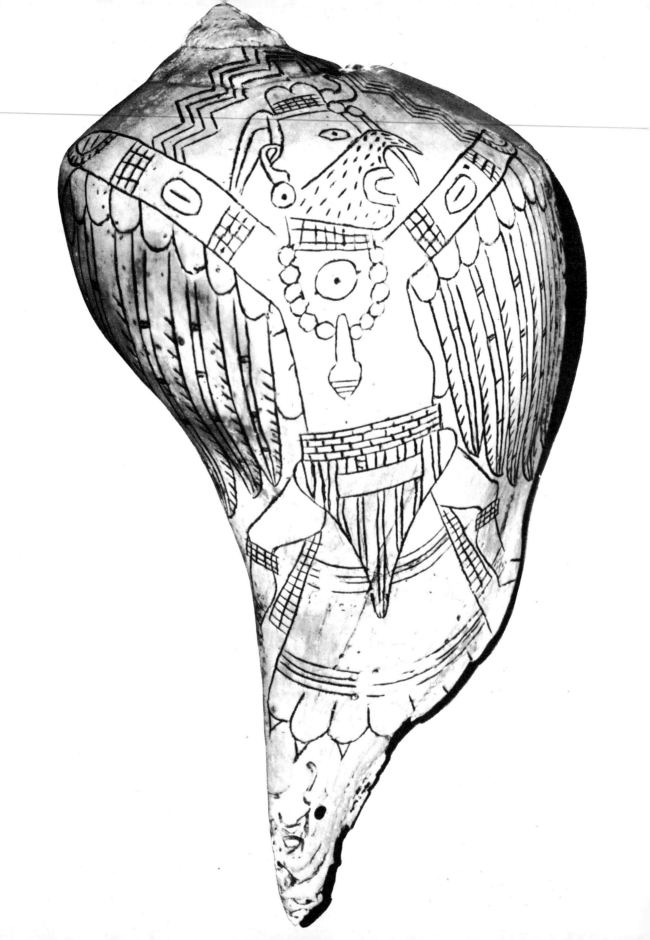

The charmed arrow

Sagimau had performed great feats against the enemies of his tribe. He had entirely routed and driven off one of the original tribes from the lakes, and came back to his residence on Lake Huron a conqueror. He was also regarded as a Manito. But, he could not feel easy while he heard of the fame and exploits of Kaubina, a great Chippewa chief and Manito in the north. Kaubina lived on a large island in Lake Superior, and was not only versed in magic himself, but had an aged female coadjutor who was a witch, and went under the name of his grandmother. She lived under Lake Superior, and took care to inform him of every thing that threatened him.

Sagimau determined to measure strength with him. He accordingly thought much about him. One night he dreamed that there was a certain head of a lance, which, if it could be procured, would give him sway over other tribes. This treasure was in the possession of a certain beautiful and majestic eagle, to whom all other birds owed obedience, and who, in consequence of having this weapon, was acknowledged king of birds. The lance was, however, seldom seen, even by those most intimate with the owner. The seer of the village dreamed the same dream. It was much talked about, and made much noise. Sagimau determined to seek for it, as it would make him the greatest hero in the world. He thought he would first go and see Kaubina, and endeavour to deceive him, or try his skill in necromancy. But he resolved to proceed by stratagem. After several days' travel he crossed the neck of land separating the two great waters, and reached the banks of Lake Superior, opposite a large island, which is now called Grand Island. Here Kaubina lived. Some days before this visit, the witch came into Kaubina's lodge and requested some tobacco. But he happened to be in an ill humour, and refused her, telling her he had none. "Very well", said she, "you will see the time when you may wish you had given me some".

Meantime Sagimau was plotting against him. He resolved to carry off his youngest wife. Having no canoe to cross to the island, he asked his companions whether any of them had ever dreamed of walking in the water. One of the men answered yes. He was therefore selected to accompany him. They went into the water until it came breast high. "You must not have the least doubt", said he to the young man, "but resolve that you can walk under water. If you doubt, you will fail. They both thought strong of it, and disappeared. When about half way through the strait, they met two monsters, who looked as long as pine trees, and had glistening eyes. But they appeased them by giving them tobacco, and went on. On getting near the island, Sagimau said to his friend, you must turn yourself into a white stone on the shore, near the path where the women come to dip water. I will assume the shape of a black log of driftwood, and be floating, and thumping on the shore near by.

Kaubina had attended a feast that day, and after he got home to his lodge, complained of thirst. He requested his old wife to get him some water. "My! My!" said she, "it is dark, and why not let that one go, whom you think so much of. He then spoke to the youngest, who immediately got a flambeau, and prepared to go, having first asked the elder wife to accompany her. She declined. Dark as it was, and alone, she pursued the path to the edge of the water. She noticed the white stone, and the wood near it, and thought she had never seen them before; but if I return, thought she to herself, with such a story, without the water, they will laugh at me. She made a quick motion to dip the water, but was instantly seized by Sagimau and his companion. They drew her under the water, carried her to the main land, and proceeded one day's journey homeward, when they encamped. Meantime Kaubina waited for his expected drink of water. He at last got up and searched for her on the shore, and in the lodges, but could get no intelligence. He was distressed, and coult not rest. Next morning he renewed his search, but in vain. He invoked the name of his grandmother, with due ceremony, making the customary present of tabacco. At length she appeared, and after reminding him of his neglect of her, in her last application for the sacred weed, she revealed to him the whole plot, and also told him the means he must use to recover his lost wife. If you follow my advice, said she, you will get her back in a friendly way, and without bloodshed. Kaubina obeyed the injunctions of the witch. He carried with him a number of young men, and overtook Sagimau at his first night's encampment. When the latter saw him, he assumed a smiling aspect, and came forward and offered his hand. It was accepted. They then sat down and smoked. After this Kaubina said, why did you take my wife. It was only, Sagimau replied, to see how great a Manito you were. Here she is—take her. Now that I know your qualities, we will live in peace. Each concealed the deep hostility he entertained for the other. They parted in peace.

After the interview, Sagimau sent his warriors home to Lake Michigan. He determined to remain in the country and seek the charmed arrow. For this purpose he retired to a remote wood, and transformed himself into a dead moose, which appeared as if the carcass had lain a long period, for worms were in its eyes and nostrils. Very soon eagles, hawks, crows, and other birds of prey, flocked to the carcass. But the skin was so hard and tough that they could not penetrate it with their bills. At length they said, let us go and call Waub We Nonga to come and cut a hole for us with his lance. Ze Ghe Nhiew offered to go, but having been told that the dead moose was Sagimau, flew back affrighted. The birds renewed their attempt to pierce the hide, but without success. They then repeated their request to the while vulture-eagle. The latter returned the same wary reply, fearful it was the stratagem of the Manito Sagimau; but when appealed to the third time, with the assurance that worms were in the eyes and nostrils of the carcass, he consented. All the birds were seated around the carcass, eager for the feast. When they heard the sweeping noise of the wings of Waub-we-nonga, the king of the birds, they made a cry of joy. He viewed the carcass from a distance. Two birds older than the rest, screamed out to him to come and cut the skin. He advanced cautiously, and gave a blow, but to no effect, the lance bounded back from the tough hide. The birds set up a loud scream, desiring that he would renew the effort. He

We must now return to Kaubina. When he had recovered his wife, he went did so, and drove the lance in, about a foot. Sagamau immediately caught hold of it and wrenched it from the bird. He instantly resumed his human form and commenced his return to his country. The great bird followed him, entreating him to give it back, and promising, on compliance, that he would grant him any thing that he might desire. Sagimau sternly refused. He knew that it contained magic virtues by which he could accomplish all his purposes, one of the first of which was, to overthrow Kaubina. This resolution he firmly maintained, although the bird followed him all the way back, flying from tree to tree, and renewing its solicitations.

Sagimau had no sooner reached his village with this trophy, than he commenced gathering all the tobacco he could, as presents to the different spirits of the land, whom he deemed it necessary to appease, in consequence of the deception he had used in wrongfully getting possession of the arrow. This sacred offering he carefully put up in cedar bags, and then commenced a journey to such places as he knew they inhabited, to leave his offering, and to obtain the permission of the Manitoes to retain his trophy. He travelled the whole circuit of Lake Michigan, and then went across to Lake Huron, visiting every high place and waterfall, celebrated as the residence of spirits. But he was unfavorably received. None of the spirits would accept his offerings. Every spirit he asked replied, "Waub-we-nonga has passed before you with his complaints, accusing you of a theft, and requesting that the arrow be returned to its lawful owner. We cannot, therefore, hear you. He who has stolen shall again be stolen from." The very same words were used by each. The last spirit he applied to lived in a cleft, on a high point of rock, surrounded by woods, on the summit of the island called Mishinimakinong. He added this sentence. "Hlox has cursed you." Thus foiled at every point, he returned home with all his tobacco. He called all his *jossakeeds*, and medicine-men, and jugglers together, and laid the gift before them, requesting their advice in this emergency. He asked each one to tell him whether his skill could designate the spirit which was meant by that outlandish word uttered on the island. One of the oldest men said, "It has been revealed to me, by my guardian spirit, in a dream. It is the name of a witch living in the bottom of Lake Superior; she is a relative of Waubwenonga." Not another word was uttered in the council. Silently they smoked out their pipes, and silently they returned to their lodges.

back directly to his lodge on the island, and with due ceremony invoked the counsel and aid of his grandmother. For this purpose he erected a *pointed* lodge, and covered it close around with bark. He took nothing in with him but his drum, medicine sack, and rattles. After singing for some time, he heard a noise under ground, and the woman appeared. "My grandson", said she, "I am made acquainted with your wishes. Your enemy seeks your blood. Sagimau has obtained the great war bird's arrow, and is preparing the sacred gift of our country (tobacco) to appease the spirits, and obtain their permission to use it. If he obtains his wishes, he will prevail. But I will use all my power to circumvent him. I have a firm friend among the guardian spirits of our nation, who lives on an island toward the south. Waubwenonga himself is my relation. You may rely upon my power. In nine days I shall reappear." At the end of that time she fulfilled her promise, and told him to watch, and that at such a time his enemy would come against him with a large war party in canoes.

In the meantine Sagimau had visited the spirits, and failed in his design. He would have remained at home, after the result of his council with the old men and sages, had he not continued to hear of the exploits of Kaubina, who was making excursions toward the southwest, and driving back all the tribes who lived on the great lake. He was not only goaded on by envy of his fame, but he thought him the cause of the spirits not accepting his tobacco, and thus rendering useless in his hands the sacred arrow. He mustered a large war party and set off in canoes for the north, for the purpose of attacking the Odjibwas. His old men tried to dissuade him from this expedition, but were not heeded. When the party reached the Great Sand Dunes, Sagimau dreamed that he saw Kaubina on an island, and took him prisoner. He was, therefore, assured of success, and went boldly on. They crossed over to the island to watch the movements of Kaubina, who, at this time, had his village on the main land. This was revealed to the latter by his grandmother, who declared the bloody intentions of the enemy. Kaubina appeared in a moment to forget this advice, for he said to his wife, "Come, let us go over to the island for basswood bark". "Why", said she, "have you not just told me that Sagimau was watching there?" "Well", said he, "I am not afraid. I would have gone if I had not heard this account, and I will go now". While crossing the bay in his canoe, he directed his wife to land him alone, and push out her canoe from the shore, and rest there, so that if any accident occurred, she might immediately cross and arouse the warriors. He directed her, the moment she reached his lodge, to take out his medicine sack, and his fighting skin, (wich was made out of a large bear skin), and to spread out the latter ready for him, when he arrived, so that he could slip it on in an instant, as he relied on its magic virtues to ensure him an easy victory. Shortly after landing him, while resting on her paddles, she heard the sa-sakwan, or war whoop. She immediately paddled for the village, and gave the alarm.

It turned out that when Kaubina landed from the canoe, he stepped ashore near the ambush of Sagimau's party, who arose to a man and instantly made him a prisoner. They immediately tied him to a tree, and pushed over to the main land to secure the village before the alarm spread. They landed very expeditiously, and getting behind the village, approached from that part. The fight had but just commenced when Kaubina appeared. He had been released by Hlox, and invoking his spirit, flew to the rescue of his people. He found his fighting skin ready, and slipping it on hastily, he now felt himself invulnerable. He then cried out to his adversary and challenged him to single combat. Sagimau did not decline. "Here am I", said he. "I defy you". They closed instantly. Blow was answered with blow, without any apparent advantage to either, till about midday, when Sagimau began to give out. He appealed to Kaubina, saying, "My elder brother, it is enough!" (nesia me-a-me-nik). No answer was returned, but the reinvigorated blows of his rival and adversary. Kaubina fought with the rage of a demon, and soon after the scalp of Sagimau was flying in the air. Nearly the whole Ottowa party fell with him. It is said the arrow which Sagimau either forgot to use, or was mysteriously withheld from using, was lost in this combat, and returned to the spirit of the King of the Birds who owned it.

Shawondasee

Mudjekewis and nine brothers conquered the Mammoth Bear, and obtained the Sacred Belt of Wampum, the great object of previous warlike enterprise, and the great means of happiness to men. The chief honour of this achievement was awarded to Mudjekewis, the youngest of the ten, who received the government of the West Winds. He is therefore called Kabeyun, the father of the winds. To his son, Wabun, he gave the East; to Shawondasee, the south, and to Kabibonokka, the North. Manabozho, being an illegitimate son, was left unprovided. When he grew up, and obtained the secret of his birth, he went to war against his father, Kabeyun, and having brought the latter to terms, he received the government of the Northwest Winds, ruling jointly with his brother Kabibonokka the tempests from that quarter of the heavens.

Shawondasee is represented as an affluent, plethoric old man, who has grown unwieldy from repletion, and seldom moves. He keeps his eyes steadfastly fixed on the north. When he sighs, in autumn, we have those balmy southern airs, which communicate warmth and delight over the northern hemisphere, and make the *Indian Summer.*

One day, while gazing toward the north, he beheld a beautiful young woman of slender and majestic form, standing on the plains. She appeared in the same place for several days, but what most attracted his admiration, was her bright and flowing locks of yellow hair. Ever dilatory, however, he contented himself with gazing. At length he saw, or fancied he saw, her head enveloped in a pure white mass like snow. This excited his jealousy toward his brother Kabibonokka, and he threw out a succession of short and rapid sighs— when lo! the air was filled with light filaments of a silvery hue, but the object of his affections had for ever vanished. In reality, the southern airs had blown off the finewinged seed-vessels of the prairie dandelion.

"My son", said the narrator, "it is not wise to differ in our tastes from other people; nor ought we to put off, through slothfulness, what is best done at once. Hat Shawondasee conformed to the tastes of his countrymen, he would not have been an admirer of *yellow* hair; and if he had evinced a proper activity in his youth, his mind would not have run flower-gathering in his age.

The linnet and eagle

The birds met together one day, to try which could fly the highest. Some flew up very swift, but soon god tired, and were passed by others of stronger wing. But the eagle went up beyond them all, and was ready to claim the victory, when the gray linnet, a very small bird, flew from the eagle's back, where it had perched unperceived, and being fresh and unexhausted, succeeded in going the highest. When the birds came down, and met in council to award the prize, it was given to the eagle, because that bird had not only gone up nearer to the sun than any of the larger birds, but it had carried the linnet on its back.

Hence the feathers of the eagle are esteemed the most honourable marks for a warrior, as it is not only considered the bravest bird, but also endowed with strength to soar the highest.

The moose
and woodpecker

After Manabozho had killed the Prince of Serpents, he was living in a state of great want, completely deserted by his powers, as a deity, and not able to procure the ordinary means of subsistence. He was at this time living with his wife and children, in a remote part of the country, where he could get no game. He was miserably poor. It was winter, and he had not the common Indian comforts.

He said to his wife, one day, I will go out a walking, and see if I cannot find some lodges. After walking some time he saw a lodge at a distance. The children were playing at the door. When they saw him approaching they ran into the lodge, and told their parents that Manabozho was coming. It was the residence of the large redheaded Woodpecker. He came to the lodge door and asked him to enter. He did so. After some time, the Woodpecker, who was a magician, said to his wife, Have you nothing to give Manabozho, he must be hungry. She answered, No. In the centre of the lodge stood a large white tamarack tree. The Woodpecker flew on to it, and commenced going up, turning his head on each side of the tree, and every now and then driving in his

189

bill. At last he drew something out of the tree, and threw it down, when, behold! a fine, fat raccoon on the ground. He drew out six or seven more. He then descended, and told his wife to prepare them. Manabozho, he said, this is the only thing we eat. What else can we give you? It is very good, replied Manabozho. They smoked their pipes and conversed with each other. After eating, the great spirit-chief got ready to go home. The Woodpecker said to his wife, Give him the remaining raccoons to take home for his children. In the act of leaving the lodge he dropped intentionally one of his mittens, which was soon after observed. Run, said the Woodpecker to his eldest son, and give it to him. But don't give it into his hand; throw it at him, for there is no knowing him, he acts so curiously. The boy did as he was bid. Nemesho (my grandfather), said he, as he came up to him, you have left one of your mittens— here it is. Yes, said he, affecting to be ignorant of the circumstance, it is so. But don't throw it, you will soil it on the snow. The lad, however, threw it, and was about to return. List, said Manabozho, is that all you eat,—do you eat nothing else with the raccoon. No, replied the young Woodpecker. Tell your father, he answered, to come and visit me, and let him bring a sack. I will give him what he shall eat with his raccoon meat. When the young one reported this to his father, the old man turned up his nose at the invitation. What does the old fellow think he has got! exclaimed he.

Some time after the Woodpecker went to pay a visit to Manabozho. He was received with the usual attention. It had been the boast of Manabozho, in former days, that he could do what any other being in the creation could, whether man or animal. He affected to have the sagacity of all animals, to understand their language, and to be capable of exactly imitating it. And in his visits to men, it was his custom to return, exactly, the treatment he had received. He was very ceremonious in following the very voice and manner of his entertainers. The Woodpecker had no sooner entered his lodge, therefore, than he commenced playing the mimic. He had previously directed his wife to change his lodge, so as to enclose a large dry tamarack tree. What can I give you, said he to the Woodpecker; but as we eat, so shall you eat. He then put a long piece of bone in his nose, in imitation of the bill of this bird, and jumping on the tamarack tree, attempted to climb it, doing as he had seen the Woodpecker do. He turned his head first on one side, then on the other. He made awkward efforts to ascend, but continually slipped down. He struck the tree with the bone in his nose, until at last he drove it so far up his nostrils that the blood began to flow, and he fell down senseless at the foot of the tree. The Woodpecker started after his drum and rattle to restore him, and having not them, succeeded in bringing him to. As soon as he came to his senses, he began to lay the blame of his failure to his wife, saying to his guest, Nemesho, it is this woman relation of yours,—*she* is the cause of my not succeeding. She has rendered me a worthless fellow. Before I took her I could also get raccoons. The Woodpecker said nothing, but flying on the tree, drew out several fine raccoons. Here, said he, this is the way *we* do, and left him with apparent contempt.

Severe weather continued, and Manabozho still suffered for the want of food. One day he walked out, and came to a lodge, which was occupied by the Moose (Möz). The young Mozonsug (diminutive form, plural number, of the noun Möz) saw him and told their father Manabozho was at the door. He told them to invite him in. Being seated they entered into conversation. At last the Moose said, What shall we give Manabozho to eat? We have nothing. His wife was seated with her back toward him, making garters. He walked up to her, and untying the covering of the armlet from her back, cut off a large piece of flesh from the square of her shoulder. He then put some medicine on it, which immediately healed the wound. The skin did not even appear to have been broken, and his wife was so little affected by it, that she did not so much as leave off her work, till he told her to prepare the flesh for eating. Manabozho, said he, this is all we eat, and it is all we can give you.

After they had finished eating Manabozho set out for home, but intentionally, as before, dropped one of his *minjekawun*, or mittens. One of the young Moose took it to him, telling him that his father had sent him with it. He had been cautioned not to hand it to him, but to throw it at him. Having done so, contrary to the remonstrance of Manabozho, he was going back when the latter cried out Bakah! Bakah! (Stop! Stop!). Is *that* the only kind of meat you eat? Tell me. Yes, answered the young man, that is all, we have nothing else. Tell your father, he replied, to come and visit me, and I will give him what you shall eat with your meat. The old Moose listened to this message with indignity. I wonder what he thinks he has got, poor fellow!

He was bound, however, to obey the invitation, and went accordingly, taking along a cedar sack, for he had been told to bring one. Manabozho received him in the same manner he had himself been received—repeating the same remarks, and attempted to supply the lack of food in the same manner.

To this end he had requested his wife to busy herself in making garters. He arose and untied the covering of her back as he had seen the Moose do. He then cut her back shockingly, paying no attention to her cries or resistance, until he saw her fall down, from the loss of blood. Manabozho, said the Moose, you are killing your wife. He immediately ran for his drum and rattle, and restored her to life by his skill. He had no sooner done this than Manabozho began to lay the blame of his ill success on his wife. Why, Nemesho, said he, this woman, this relation of yours—she is making me a most worthless fellow. Formerly, I procured my meat in this way. But now I can accomplish nothing.

The Moose then cut large pieces of flesh off his own thighs, without the least injury to himself, and gave them to Manabozho, saying with a contemptuous air, this is the way *we* do. He then left the lodge.

After these visits Manabozho was sitting pensively in his lodge one day, with his head down. He heard the wind whistling around it, and thought, by attentively listening, he could hear the voice of some one speaking to him. It seemed to say to him; Great chief, why are you sorrowful. Am not I your friend—your guardian Spirit? He immediately took up his rattle, and without leaving his sitting posture, began to sing the chant which at the close of every stanza has the chorus of "Whaw Lay Le Aw." When he had devoted a long time to this chant, he laid his rattle aside, and determined to fast. For this purpose he went to a cave, and built a very small fire near which he laid down, first telling his wife, that neither she nor the children must come near him, till he had finished his fast. At the end of seven days he came back to the lodge, pale and emaciated. His wife in the meantime had dug through the snow, and got a small quantity of the root called truffles. These she boiled and set before him. When he had finished his repast, he took his large bow and bent it. Then placing a strong arrow to the string, he drew it back, and sent the arrow, with the strength of a giant, through the side of his bark lodge. There, said he to his wife, go to the outside, and you will find a large bear, shot through the heart. She did so, and found one as he had predicted.

He then sent the children out to get red willow sticks. Of these he cut off as many pieces, of equal length, as would serve to invite his friends to a feast. A red stick was sent to each one, not forgetting the Moose and the Wood-pecker.

When they arrived they were astonished to see such a profusion of meat cooked for them, at such a time of scarcity. Manabozho understood their

194

glances and felt a conscious pride in making such a display. Akewazi, said he, to one of the oldest of the party, the weather is very cold, and the snow lasts a long time. We can kill nothing now but small squirrels. And I have sent for you to help me eat some of them. The Woodpecker was the first to put a mouthful of the bear's meat to his mouth, bu he had no sooner begun to taste it, than it changed into a dry powder, and set him coughing. It appeared as bitter as ashes. The Moose felt the same effect, and began to cough. Each one, in turn, was added to the number of coughers. But they had too much sense of decorum, and respect for their entertainer, to say any thing. The meat looked very fine. They thought they would try more of it. But the more they ate, the faster they coughed and the louder became the uproar, until Manabozho, exerting his former power, which he now felt to be renewed, transformed them all into the Adjidamo, or squirrel, an animal which is still found to have the habit of barking, or coughing, whenever it sees any one approach its nest.

Iagoo

Iagoo is the name of a personage noted in Indian love for having given extravagant narrations of whatever he had seen, heard, or accomplished. It seems that he always saw extraordinary things, made extraordinary journeys, and performed extraordinary feats. He could not look out of his lodge and see things as other men did. If he described a bird, it had a most singular variety of brilliant plumage. The animals he met with were all of the monstrous kind; they had eyes like orbs of fire, and claws like hooks of steel, and could step over the top of an Indian lodge. He told of a serpent he had seen, which had hair on its neck like a mane, and feet resembling a quadruped; and if one were to take his own account of his exploits and observations, it would be difficult to decide whether his strength, his activity, or his wisdom should be most admired.

Iagoo did not appear to have been endowed with the ordinary faculties of other men. His eyes appeared to be magnifiers, and the tympanum of his ears so constructed that what appeared to common observers to be but the sound of a zephyr, to him had a far closer resemblance to the noise of thunder.

His imagination appeared to be of so exuberant a character, that he scarcely required more than a drop of water to construct an ocean, or a grain of sand to form an earth. And he had so happy an exemption from both the restraints of judgment and moral accountability, that he never found the slightest difficulty in accommodating his facts to the most enlarged credulity. Nor was his ample thirst for the marvellous ever quenched by attempts to reconcile statements the most strange, unaccountable, and preposterous.

Such was Iagoo, the Indian story-teller, whose name is associated with all that is extravagant and marvellous, and has long been established in the hunter's vocabulary as a perfect synonym for liar, and is bandied about as a familiar proverb. If a hunter or warrior, in telling his exploits, undertakes to embellish them; to overrate his merits, or in any other way to excite the incredulity of his hearers, he is liable to be rebuked with the remark, "So here we have Iagoo come again". And he seems to hold the relative rank in oral narration which our written literature awards to Baron Munchausen, Jack Falstaff, and Captain Lemuel Gulliver.

Notwithstanding all this, there are but a few scraps of his actual stories to be found. He first attracted notice by giving an account of a water lilly, a single leaf of which, he averred, was sufficient to make a petticoat and upper garments for his wife and daughter. One evening he was sitting in his lodge, on the banks of a river, and hearing the quacking of ducks on the stream, he fired through the lodge door at a venture. He killed a swan that happened to be flying by, and twenty brace of ducks in the stream. But this did not check the force of his shot; they passed on, and struck the heads of two loons, at the moment they were coming up from beneath the water, and even went beyond and killed a most extraordinary large fish called Moshkeenozha (the muscalunge). On another occasion he had killed a deer, and after skinning it, was carrying the carcass on his shoulders, when he spied some stately elks on the plain before him. He immediately gave them chase, and had run, over hill and dale, a distance of half a day's travel, before he recollected that he had the deer's carcass on his shoulders.

One day, as he was passing over a tract of *mushkeeg*, or bog-land, he saw mosquitoes of such enormous size, that he staked his reputation on the fact that a single wing of one of the insects was sufficient for a sail to his canoe, and the proboscis as big as his wife's shovel. But he was favoured with a still more extraordinary sight, in a gigantic ant, which passed him, as he was watching a beaver's lodge, dragging the entire carcass of a hare.

At another time, for he was ever seeing or doing something wonderful. he got out of smoking weed, and in going into the woods in search of some, he discovered a bunch of the red willow, or maple bush, of such a luxuriant growth, that he was industriously occupied half a day in walking round it.

Adventures of a warrior's soul

There was once a battle between the Indians, in which many were killed on both sides. Among the number was the leader of the Odjibwas, a very brave man, who had fought in many battles; but while he was shouting for victory, he received an arrow in his flesh, and fell as if dead. At last his companions *thought he was dead*, and treated him as if he were. They placed his body in a sitting posture, on the field of battle, his back being supported by a tree, and his face toward the enemies' country. They put on him his head-dress of feathers, and leaned his bow against his shoulders, for it was before the white men had brought guns for the Indians. They then left him and returned to their homes.

The warrior, however, heard and saw all they did. Although his body was deprived of muscular motion, his soul was living within it. He heard them lament his death, and felt their touch as they set him up. "They will not be so cruel as to leave me here, he thought to himself. I am certainly not dead. I have the use of my senses." But his anguish was extreme, when he saw them, one after another depart, till he was left alone among the dead. He could not move a limb, nor a muscle, and felt as if he were buried in his own body. Horrid agonies came over him. He exerted himself, but found that he had no power over his muscles. At last he appeared to leap out of himself. He first stood up, and then followed his friends. He soon overtook them, but when he arrived at their camp no one noticed him. He spoke to them, but no one answered. He seemed to be *invisible* to them, and his voice appeared to have no *sound*. Unconscious, however, of his body's being left behind, he thought their conduct most strange. He determined to follow them, and exactly imitated all they did, walking when they walked, running when they ran, sleeping when they slept. But the most unbroken silence was maintained as to his presence.

When evening came he addressed the party. "Is it possible," said he, "that you do not see me, nor hear me, nor understand me? Will you permit me to starve when you have plenty? Is there no one who recollects me?" And with similar sentiments he continued to talk to them, and to upbraid them at every stage of their homeward journey, but his words seemed to pass like the sounds of the wind.

At length they reached the village, and the women and children, and old men, came out, according to custom, to welcome the returning war party. They set up the shout of praise. Kumaudjing! kumaudjing! kumaudjing! They have met, fought, and conquered, was heard at every side. Group after group repeated the cry.

The truth, however, was soon revealed; although it caused a momentary check, it did not mar the *general* joy. The sight of scalps made every tongue vocal. A thousand inquiries were made, and he heard his own fate described, how he had fought bravely, been killed, and left among the dead.

"It is not true," replied the indignant chief, "that I was killed and left upon the field of battle. I am here. I live. I move. See me." Nobody answered. He then walked to his own lodge. He saw his wife tearing her hair, and lamenting his fate. He asked her to bind up his wounds. She made no reply. He placed his mouth close to her ear, and called for food. She did not notice it. He drew back his arm and struck her a blow. She felt nothing.

Thus foiled he determined to go back. He followed the track of the warriors. It was four days' journey. During three days he met with nothing extraordinary. On the fourth, toward evening, as he drew near the skirts of the battle field, he saw a fire in the path. He stepped on one side, but the fire had also moved its position. He crossed to the other side, but the fire was still before him. Whichever way he took, the fire appeared to bar his approach. At this moment he espied the enemy of his fortunes in the mocassin, or flat-headed snake. "My son" said the reptile, "you have heretofore been considered a brave man— but beware of this fire. It is a strong spirit. You must appease it by the sacred gift." The warrior put his hand to his side, but he had left his sack behind him. "Demon," he exclaimed, addressing the flame, "why do you bar my approach. Know that I am a spirit. I have never been defeated by my enemies, and I will not be defeated by you."

So saying, he made a sudden effort and leaped through the flames. In this effort *he awoke from his trance.* He had lain eight days on the battle field. He found himself sitting on the ground, with his back supported by a tree, and his bow leaning against his shoulder, as his friends had left him. He looked up and beheld a large Gha Niew, or war eagle, sitting in the tree, which he immediately recognised as his guardian spirit, or personal Manito. This bird had watched his body, and prevented the other birds of prey from devouring it.

He arose and stood for a few minutes, but found himself weak and emaciated. By the use of simples and such forest arts as our people are versed in, he succeeded in reaching his home. When he came near, he uttered the Sa sa kwan, or war cry, which threw the village into an uproar. But while they were debating the meaning of so unexpected a sound, the wounded chief was ushered into their midst. He related his adventures as before given. He con-cluded his narrative by telling them that it is pleasing to the spirits of the dead to have a fire lit up on their graves at night, after their burial. He gave as a reason, that it is four days' travel to the place appointed for the residence of the soul, and it requires a light every night at the place of its encampment. If the friends of the deceased neglect this rite, the spirit is compelled to build a fire for itself.

Printed by
Officine Grafiche de
Aldo Garzanti Editore, SpA
Milano

Printed in Italy